The Gentle Art of
Spiritual
Discernment

"A rare and precious read, not only because the content is deeply profound and insightful but also inspirational and wise. Simple in language and tone, it is a heart-opening invitation for accelerated spiritual growth and conscious awakening. This is a book written by that rare species of 'root' teacher, who, in our modern world, are now few and far between. The messages of these great lights convey the purest transmissions because they themselves are the very essence of their teachings: in other words, they walk their talk. Turning the pages, one experiences a level of intimacy rarely achieved in the written form. It is like talking with an old, treasured friend; a spiritual mentor. A book you will wish to keep close to hand long after you have read it."

NICOLYA CHRISTI, AUTHOR OF *LOVE, GOD & EVERYTHING*

"This book by a true spiritual master asks the fundamental questions we all need to ask—and search to answer. It opens the whole dimension of spirituality to the reader—genuine, lived spirituality, the inner authority we all need if we are to find our way in these critical times."

ERVIN LASZLO, PH.D., WHOLE SYSTEMS THEORIST,
PHILOSOPHER, AUTHOR, AND FOUNDER OF THE
CLUB OF BUDAPEST AND THE LASZLO INSTITUTE
OF NEW PARADIGM RESEARCH

"From beginning to end, Pierre Pradervand's pen poetically dances. It's like reading an epic poem without stanzas that literally pulls you in. *The Gentle Art of Spiritual Discernment* is a marvelous journey."

"A book that will serve many who are exploring their spiritual journey in their own unique and personal way."

"The reader will find so many inspirational points of guidance here, as the author outlines the simplest path to achieving the noblest goal of becoming the embodiment of divine love. Rejoice in finding your own glowing path beyond convention, beyond tradition, beyond recriminations, anger, and hate, beyond rules and regulations, as you find your own key to the mansion of your spirituality, the giant within."

"From the moment I began reading *The Gentle Art of Spiritual Discernment*, I literally could not put it down. My hungry soul drank in every word of his highly inspirational stories, examples, quotes, and teachings!"

The Gentle Art of
Spiritual
Discernment

*A Guide to Discovering
Your Personal Path*

Pierre Pradervand

Destiny Books
Rochester, Vermont

Destiny Books
One Park Street
Rochester, Vermont 05767
www.DestinyBooks.com

Text stock is SFI certified

Destiny Books is a division of Inner Traditions International

Originally published in French in 2021 under the title *Comment trouver son chemin spirituel* by Éditions Jouvence
First U.S. edition published in 2023 by Destiny Books

Cataloging-in-Publication Data for this title is available from the Library of Congress

ISBN 978-1-64411-805-4 (print)
ISBN 978-1-64411-806-1 (ebook)

Printed and bound in the United States by Lake Book Manufacturing, LLC
The text stock is SFI certified. The Sustainable Forestry Initiative® program promotes sustainable forest management.

10 9 8 7 6 5 4 3 2 1

Text design and layout by Virginia Scott Bowman
This book was typeset in Garamond Premier Pro and Gill Sans with Alverata and Minion Pro used as display typefaces

To send correspondence to the author of this book, mail a first-class letter to the author c/o Inner Traditions • Bear & Company, One Park Street, Rochester, VT 05767, and we will forward the communication, or contact the author directly at **www.pierrepradervand.com**.

I dedicate this book to
Robin and Ronald Radford, my uniquely
precious American friends.
Thank you for your special companionship
over so many years.

Contents

Foreword

Jonathan Ellerby, Ph.D.

IT IS AN HONOR TO WRITE the foreword to this book. Pierre Pradervand has blessed us before with inspiring words and works that uplift the soul, and here again, he offers us a light for the spiritual path. Personally, as an author of spiritual growth and holistic health books, I have often wondered if the world really needs another book about spiritual growth. Don't we feel like too many people are saying the same things over and over again, only in different ways? I used to think that the last thing we need is yet another book about how to be "more spiritual" and that many authors are simply too attached to their own views.

I don't feel that way any longer. As the world accelerates into what appears to be an unprecedented time of worldwide opportunity and chaos, we need every teacher, author, and wisdom keeper to step forward with the best they have to offer. In particular, I feel that our spiritual focus must be strong. In a time when human structures, systems, and simple routines are being altered and challenged on a regular basis, we can thrive by staying rooted in the changeless aspects of life and through a steady relationship with the transcendent. Spirituality is not about escaping life. It is about removing the barriers to the abundant feelings of love and connection we are born with. Spirituality is about exposing our misconceptions of life and self and living more fully with resilience, contentment, and an abiding sense of purpose to evolve in compassion, awareness, and relationship.

As more people on Earth awaken to a deep and more personal feeling of connection to life with a sense of the sacredness of our world, we will see more courageous changemakers rising up to help bring healing and hope to others. It is a simple equation we must encourage. To truly embrace questions of meaning and mystery, we must be willing to let go, to grow, and to awaken to an inner presence that is innately spiritual. Perhaps that is the heart of the work we need most: to remember that we are an expression of what we seek.

Making a commitment to a spiritual journey—to knowing Spirit in your heart, as you understand it—means allowing the path to take you somewhere and not becoming stuck in one place. Any religious practice that keeps you safe and in a prescribed place is dangerous, removed from spirituality. With or without religion, spirituality allows us to adopt a way of being that is a true adventure and an incredible way to live and find peace within. Navigating this path is not as easy as it might seem, and often our intuition is clouded by conditioning. As a result, we face a great paradox in the spiritual journey. We are seeking something we already have but need help finding it.

Finding a guide, engaging in trusted spiritual practices, and developing a sense of what to expect along the way are all invaluable investments for the spiritual journey. *The Gentle Art of Spiritual Discernment* provides just the kind of guidance our world of blossoming spiritual seekers needs. For more seasoned travelers, this book provides helpful reminders and new insights that are still vital and important regardless of one's state or stage in the process. This is an endless journey, and I welcome all the guidance and diverse perspectives I can get. I hope you do too. I also hope you will consider that your spiritual health is the foundation of all well-being for yourself and our planet. This book is a wonderful place to start!

CLAREMONT, CALIFORNIA,

JANUARY 2022

JONATHAN ELLERBY is a two-time bestselling author, speaker, teacher, coach, and consultant with a Ph.D. in comparative religion focused on Indigenous healing traditions and cross-cultural research. He has been featured in film, radio, print, and multiple event forms as an expert on mastering change, integrative wellness and resilience, mindfulness, and holistic approaches to spiritual growth. Influenced by more than three decades of ceremony and study with Indigenous traditions, and a deep relationship to Wilderness, his unique perspective has been sought after by and featured in numerous media outlets including the *New York Times,* the *Yoga Journal, Larry King Live,* the *Martha Stewart Radio Show, Readers Digest, Woman's Day,* CBS and NBC regional morning shows, and BetterTV, to name only a few.

Preface

FOR WELL OVER FIFTY-FIVE YEARS, I have traveled around this little planet, although less extensively recently, and these travels have enabled me to encounter a great variety of people, cultures, belief systems, and lifestyles. I have thus become aware that a remarkable spiritual awakening is happening, mainly, for the moment it seems, in the West. More and more people are experiencing a real need for spirituality. On the individual level, spirituality can play a key role in shaping happiness, offering meaning to life, and enabling us to find our right place in this world, which so often appears topsy-turvy. Even in the area of our health, spirituality may have some contribution to increased serenity and decreased disease.

For thousands of years, religion has held the monopoly on spirituality and has dictated the lifestyles of adherents, down to the smallest details, which has, in some cases, imprisoned them in a shackle of forbidden behavior and stripped life of the slightest residue of joy. Consequently, many people in the West have rejected organized religion, and church attendance has fallen drastically.

But it is difficult to live in a world void of meaning, and

the apparent disappearance of the main Christian churches in Western Europe and increasingly also in North America have opened up a need for spiritual guidance. Thanks to the shrinking of the world—in part due to tourism, not to mention the incredible role played by the Internet—people have access to a multitude of spiritual paths, which was inconceivable only a few years ago. This spiritual supermarket offers the best and the worst, from profound and authentic spiritual teachings that help students to progress to pseudo-gurus who offer retreats at island paradises and promote teachings that are a bizarre cocktail of New Age theories and messages one wonders where on Earth they came from. In Japan, one can even rent the services of a Buddhist monk, and one of the best Swiss dailies, *Le Temps,* asks if we are not witnessing the "uberization" of spirituality.

All these trends are but a pale reflection of the incredible confusion we are familiar with in so many areas.

Perhaps we can do better.

Byron Katie, one of the most outstanding authorities worldwide in the field of personal development, had already stated about a generation ago that the number one problem in the world was not wars, hunger, or conflicts of all sorts. It was *confusion.* And it is true that confusion is a huge challenge in so, so many areas—both for collective and individual behavior.

Hence, this modest presentation aims at offering a short guide for those embarking on a spiritual search or refining the path on which they have already started, to see more clearly, to avoid pitfalls, to open their horizons, and to choose the path that corresponds best to what they are really seeking in life. From time to time, I have inserted a question in bold italics, which I suggest you ponder before you continue.

Blessing for Spiritual Seekers

We are in a period of unprecedented, challenging, and exciting change. In all areas, old structures are falling away or being challenged, including in the field of religion and spirituality. More and more people are undertaking an individual spiritual quest for their right spiritual niche. This blessing is for them.

I bless all those who are on an honest spiritual quest.

I bless them in their courage to break away from old moorings that keep them in stagnant waters and to embark onto the unchartered territories of their soul and the moving seas of spiritual adventure.

I bless them in their firm determination to continue seeking until they find the pearl of great price and the "peace that passes all understanding."

I bless them, above all else, in their ability to be true to themselves, wherever it may take them, and to hold firm to their vision whatever the pressures from family, friends, religious bodies, and "authorities" of all sorts to conform.

1

The Starting Point

Well begun is half done.

—ATTRIBUTED TO ARISTOTLE

AFTER THOUSANDS OF PEOPLE SHARED their desire to progress in my workshops and many, many other settings, not to mention my own much longer personal road, my vision of a good point of departure can be summed up with this sentence of Polonius in *Hamlet* by Shakespeare: "This above all: to thinc own self be true, and it must follow, as the night the day, thou canst not then be false to any man."

One of the most popular texts of my workshops touches just on this theme. It is simply entitled "Integrity" and has helped countless people live better lives, and it is certainly one of the foundation stones of my own existence. It is maybe the most fundamental step for any person embarking on a spiritual path.

INTEGRITY

Integrity is a quality of being. It means holding on at all times to your highest sense of truth and your own vision, whatever the cost may be. It consists in resonating with the most intimate fiber of your being and enjoins us not to withdraw one inch, whatever the prestige or authority of the person or institution opposing us—not out of obstinacy but because of the quiet courage of an inner voice that says: "This above all: to thine own self be true."

Integrity means following at all times one's highest sense of what is right, whatever the consequences may be, however solitary your path, and however loud the taunts and the mockeries of the crowd and the Pharisees.

Following your integrity means "speaking truth to power," as the Quaker wisdom goes, even when silence would better serve your interests. It means hanging on to truth when all those surrounding accept compromises or pretend that it's not really important. It means being unflinching and firm when others disappear in the underground shelters of their fears and timidity.

Integrity means refusing to dilute one's inner sense of truthfulness, be it to satisfy, appease, or gain the approval of one's beloved.

Above all, integrity means refusing to cheat yourself, lie to yourself, or abide in the shade of half-truths. You can lie to others—even deceive them—and be forgiven. But when you lie to yourself, who is there to forgive you? After a defeat of this sort, who will help you get up again? Even if you are sufficiently ignorant to let yourself indulge in the supreme absurdity of deceiving yourself, will not your inner strength abandon the ship of one who voluntarily scuttles it in that manner? In such moments, grace alone can save you.

To deceive oneself kills the discernment that is the basis of honest judgments and meaningful choices. To consciously avoid what one knows to be true or to lie to oneself is the sin against the spirit, which resides deep down in each one of us.

Integrity, as the most intimate substance of our being, constitutes the marrow of our identity and the foundation of all our qualities, starting with love. It is the woof on which we weave the exquisite textures of our existence, creating a tapestry. No woof, no tapestry. When integrity is married to love in a joyful dance, it forms the perfect couple, and our existence becomes a celebration of life.

So when winds and tempests howl or when a tempter whispers that "a compromise is absolutely essential" and attempts to make us avoid the challenges we need to grow and stay awake, let us at all costs hold on firmly to that inner foundation, our integrity—for in it resides true life.

Q *Another point of departure concerns our basic beliefs about the universe. Ask yourself: Do I believe the universe is born of chance and run by chance, or that it is governed by a benevolent entity and predictable laws?*

A great British astronomer of the last century suggested that the probability that the big bang was born of chance was equivalent to having a hurricane blow over a junk heap and leave behind a brand-new 747. Not a very likely event! Personally, I believe that the universe is entirely run by a fundamental law of harmony, which cannot be understood intellectually, for the wealth and the complexity of the universe are so stunning no human mind can grasp them. Especially on the spiritual level, it is first of all the heart (and to a lesser degree the body) that is capable of really integrating this other reality of the spiritual plane, which is on the mystical level, beyond the rational plane.

And here I would like to share an experience I had that has become the foundation of my belief. It happened many years ago and convinced me that a fundamental law of love runs absolutely everything, whatever the contrary appearances on the material level. This major learning experience is the point of departure on which I have based my whole life, starting with my spirituality. It is my fundamental spiritual anchor.

Many years ago, I was attending a meeting of the Association Internationale 6-S in the city of Ouahigouya in northern Burkina Faso, a country in West Africa. This association, of which I was one of the co-founders in the late seventies, was the largest grassroots peasant farmers organization on the continent. The last day of the meeting I caught dysentery. I spent the last afternoon we had off taking care of myself, healing myself by purely spiritual means. By the evening, the problem seemed to have disappeared, but the next day going to the airport, it started again.

On the plane I diligently worked with my spiritual affirmations and texts, trying to heal myself. I was sitting next to an unaccompanied young boy around eight or nine years old. The flight attendant taking care of him was the incarnation of kindness. So warm, so gentle, constantly coming to check if he was OK—one could have taken her for his mother. She came and spoke to him with such tenderness that I felt for this woman a kind of cosmic gratitude that enveloped me entirely.

Suddenly, I had an out-of-body experience. I was projected out of this plane of existence and time into a space where there was only the most incredible feeling of a universal, all-encompassing, infinitely tender love. No thinking was involved at all, only feeling. Pierre Pradervand—and hence any trace of my ego—had completely disappeared. Any human sense of existing as a person had radically disappeared, totally vanished. My mind, my intellect had dissipated completely.

For an indeterminate moment (as we were out of time), the divine consciousness *was* my consciousness, and there was none other. Love was the only power, substance, presence, reality, law, knowledge, cause, and effect of everything. *Besides that, there was nothing.* The whole experience was totally on the level of feeling, and for this reason, it became the most powerful, moving, and surprising moment of my whole life.

Suddenly, I snapped out of this state and was back in my seat. I felt something moving in my bowels, and in a matter of seconds, the dysentery had disappeared. But the real healing, which transformed my whole life, was that vision of existence and of a universe governed by love, which took me many years to integrate.

Today, I have the deep conviction that the only thing that really matters (at least for me) is to grow in love—and here I am still in kindergarten. But the aim is perfectly clear: one day to think, speak, and act with love, to look at all with the eyes of love, to feel only love. That is my spiritual objective and my path. I believe that the meaning of the major upheavals the planet is undergoing today is to help us go beyond the tired, old, rather pathetic win-lose model and to move toward a win-win world that works for all, the environment included. And we will manage, because it is a loving providence beyond anything we can even dream of that is pulling the strings.

Who or What Is God?

Many years ago, I was living in Senegal, West Africa. I lived on a beach between two shanty towns. I was on very friendly terms with the son of the imam of one of the two towns, and one Sunday afternoon I decided I would go to the imam's home (a small wooden shack built on the sand) and ask him how Islam defined God. At the time I was a member of a small Christian movement that claimed to represent the highest if not ultimate revelation of truth, so I was cocksure that I had the "highest" views on the topic.

As I strode across the beach to Imam Sall's little shack, my frame of mind closely reflected the Japanese proverb that states: "It is difficult to describe the vast horizons of the ocean to the little frog sitting at the bottom of his well." I was the little frog trapped in a well of spiritual smugness—not exactly the ideal state of mind for a spiritual explorer, which I eventually became. Imam Sall greeted me with his usual kindness and gentleness, and after the customary exchange, I sat down and asked him my question: How does Islam define God?

The little frog in me was in for the surprise of his life when he said: "Pierre, if you took the water of all the oceans and seas, all the rivers and lakes and streams of the world as ink, if you took all the branches of all the trees on the planet as pens, you could not write out all the names of God." No words can encompass something as extraordinary, as unfathomable as the godhead. And then he added: "You know, Pierre, you are a better Muslim than most of the Muslims who surround me." By that he meant that I did not drink alcohol, I didn't chase women, and I was generous with my giving.

The poet Edwin Markham wrote a lovely little ditty, which goes:

> He drew a circle that shut me out—
> Heretic, rebel, a thing to flout.
> But Love and I had the wit to win.
> We drew a circle and took him in.

Thank you, Imam Sall, for teaching me one of the great lessons of my life. Thank you, Imam Sall, for including me.

In all cases, seeking one's spiritual path demands an immense discernment, and this will be one of the aims of this little book: to help you develop a sharp discernment that will help you avoid being misled down the wrong path. As Mariana Caplan writes in her lucid study *Eyes Wide Open*: "Discernment doesn't prevent us from making errors, but it does help us learn life's lessons more clearly and quickly, turn challenges into opportunities, and avoid unnecessary obstacles" (Caplan 2009).

AN IMPORTANT PRECISION

It is important to point out right from the beginning that spirituality is a highly personal affair. No one can take the unique path that will be yours (unless you copy and paste someone else's version, be it a teacher's or a school's) or give you the exact understanding that will be yours to develop by yourself. Hence, this book will not offer you a spiritual Google map to find your destination. Various teachings, traditions, and spiritual teachers will, of course, be invaluable, sometimes even indispensable, but you alone are capable of interpreting the lessons that are adapted to your situation or your unique path. If someone attempts or wishes to propose to you that his or her map or truth is the right one, be careful. You alone can find it, for you alone really know what you are seeking and the amount of effort, time, energy, resources you are ready to invest in this search. Your only guide—but what a wise and adequate guide—is your own heart.

All I would say is that the heart of this path will be the search for the sacred, for I believe the sacred is the heart of all authentic spiritual experience. For many spiritual teachers and teachings, the search for the sacred is simply the center of life, period. Mary Baker Eddy, a pioneer of American spiritual research in North America in the nineteenth century, used to say: "All is infinite Mind and its infinite manifestation." You can replace Mind by Love or Spirit—for her it was the same reality. They are all synonyms she used to define God. One of the most exciting and surprising discoveries of your path will be that the sacred, the Divine, is literally everywhere, albeit in disguises that make it completely unrecognizable. In a really outstanding book on these issues, Jonathan Ellerby, speaking of an experience that is completely out of the ordinary, writes: "As I looked around, not only did I see and feel that all things were from the divine Source, but I saw and felt that all things *were* Divine. Every stone, every breath of wind, every thought and every moment—everything is sacred" (Ellerby 2009).

If you wish to preserve both your freedom and your authentic identity, you will have to make your own choices.

Thus, the sacred is something one perceives essentially with the heart and the senses, so neglected in the Western tradition, which is so focused on the intellect and "correct" theological definitions. In my experience of infinite love on my plane ride from Burkina Faso, absolutely everything was taking place on the level of the heart, of feeling. The mental, intellectual planes had totally disappeared, were simply nonexistent.

No one can tell you which path you should follow, and if someone or a movement makes such a claim, run away at top speed, for it is an outright abuse of power. I write from experience, as for a long period in my life I submitted to a rigorous spiritual teaching, and the results were catastrophic.

Some people choose to rely on a spiritual master, a spiritual movement, or (like me for a time) a teaching giving very specific guidelines on how to live all aspects of one's life, whereas others are much more eclectic in their spiritual choices.

Q *Do I feel capable of making an autonomous choice in selecting my spiritual path?*

Whether you choose to adopt a specific teaching, follow a spiritual master, or be your own independent spiritual thinker, as I am now, it is essential that it really be an autonomous choice that corresponds to what your heart tells you, not your head—however intellectually seductive a potential path may be to you.

Even before choosing your path, it is essential to have a clear idea of who you are, what your priority is, and what your motivation is.

Q *Who am I really?*

This is not a book about your self-image, but it is essential that you have at least some awareness of who you really are if you wish to start following a spiritual path with at least some sense of your destination. For instance, if you believe yourself to be an essentially material being inhabited by a soul that comes from some mysterious place, at least at the beginning, your path will be very different from someone who believes she consciously chose her present incarnation to learn certain lessons that she will take with her once she has left this fabulous but temporary vehicle called the body.

Q *What is my main priority in life? What am I really seeking?*

Do you want to find personal serenity? Help to build a win-win world that works for all? Prepare for your next reincarnation? Get ahead in life socially and materially? (I doubt many in this last category would be reading this book!) Whatever your reply, it is important to realize that rare are the spiritual journeys of a long duration that do not pass through their Valley of Baca (valley of weeping or tears)—mine lasted quite a few years. (And today I say a resounding thank you because I needed a really thorough inner cleansing and I got it—with 100 percent pure bleach!)

Q *What is the deep motivation of my spiritual research?*

Is it inner peace? A life of service? Consecrating yourself more to spiritual pursuits? Expressing unconditional love? The elevation of the collective level of consciousness? For me the latter is the most important pursuit on Earth today, as ultimately our survival depends on this more than anything else. The search for a purely individual salvation is seen more and more as the heritage of a dualist past, which has haunted us for so long.

Dualism and Nondualism

The religions and spiritual teachings of humanity can be classified as either dualist or nondualist.

The very great majority, especially the three Middle Eastern and Western religions (Judaism, Christianity, and Islam), are dualist. To use a very simple metaphor, in the dualist vision, God is seen as sitting at the top of a tall mountain, which the believer has to climb, sometimes very painfully, scratching his knees, holding on as best he can to the bushes and shrubs, hoping one day to reach the top. And in the protestant Calvinism of my childhood, as an additional touch of sadism, the mountain was covered with soap. Each Sunday, the preacher would read a notorious "Declaration of Sins," which was read as an immense reprimand and which stated, among other pronouncements, that we were "born in sin, inclined toward evil, and incapable by ourselves of any good"! This blow with a cruel theological bludgeon made us slide back a few feet, and we started all over again on Monday, knowing that the following Sunday we would have to go through the same icy shower. In numerous dualistic approaches, salvation is something one must earn, which implies material sacrifices and other good works, numerous merits, offerings, pilgrimages, and many other similar actions.

In nondualism, you are already at the top of the mountain, one with the Source, with the Divine, and only the fog prevents you from seeing you have already reached your destination. So the needed effort is simply to blow away the fog, which is why in nondual approaches one speaks of illumination and not of climbing the mountain. It is infinitely more restful, as you have already arrived. But it also implies major efforts and great perseverance over many years to overcome the suggestions of the mind that "you are not doing enough." Discipline is just as necessary, but it is not as heavy, and especially, it is more joyful.

WHEN SPIRITUALITY BECOMES BIG BUSINESS

The capacity of consumer society to co-opt absolutely everything is simply phenomenal, and the field of spirituality has become a very lucrative business. If you have the money, you can travel to India for a personal meeting with a famous guru in his ashram, or to Egypt for a unique experience in the tomb of a pharaoh, or to Brazil or Bali to encounter a shaman. The list is almost endless. In India alone, the "spirituality" business, which involves only a small fraction of the population, is estimated at $30 billion, while the market for yoga in the United States alone is worth $50 billion.

The temptation to corrupt an authentic spiritual approach and cash in on it is very great, and many are those who are beguiled by these spiritual hucksters. Once more, it follows that great discernment is necessary to avoid falling prey to any one of these numerous spiritual scams. As Caplan writes, the organizations, communities, and teachers characterized by a high degree of integrity are not legion.

One exception is certainly the Quakers or Society of Friends, as they are also called—a spiritual movement with which I feel a deep affinity and whose meetings I have attended both in the United States and Europe. Quaker meetings are the incarnation of their convictions: they are usually held in circles, in silence, with someone occasionally getting up to communicate a very brief message they feel impelled to share. That's all. Total sobriety. These meetings are still very much alive, especially in English-speaking countries, though quite a few also take place in European cities.

WHO ARE THE QUAKERS?

Founded by Englishman George Fox (1624–1691), Quakerism, or the Society of Friends, is one of the most original movements in the history of Christianity and unquestionably one of the closest to the original teachings of Jesus. These teachings were later deeply distorted by the Christian church, as the great French writer of the last century, Jacques Ellul, so clearly shows in his groundbreaking book *The Subversion of Christianity.*

Of very modest origins, Fox was apprenticed first to a cobbler and then worked for some time as a shepherd. This last experience developed in him an immense desire to live simply and with great humility, and this simplicity has always been one of the marked characteristics of the Quaker way of life. Fox was profoundly shocked by the grandiose style of the then dominant Anglican church of that period, which had distanced itself so much from the teachings of Christ.

He developed two ideas, which were radical for that period, one being that all people carry a divine spark within themselves, hence that each one could have direct contact with the Divine. He therefore asserted that there was no need for a quasi-omnipotent clergy nor for the numerous sacraments of the time. He also promoted the idea that all human beings are equal, and for this reason the Quakers did not take off their hats for the noble class, which was shocking for the times. Furthermore, he defended the most shocking idea at the time: that women have a soul and thus are equal to men and so could officiate in religious meetings. His radical ideas caused him to be imprisoned on different occasions.

The Quakers also always practiced radical nonviolence, refusing to participate in armed conflicts, and for this they have frequently been met with opposition from the powers that be. Many of Fox's followers emigrated to the United States under the leadership of a British Quaker nobleman, William Penn, hence the state of Pennsylvania is named in his honor. There is a lovely anecdote that reveals so beautifully the Quaker approach to ethics based on one's sense of inner freedom. Penn carried a sword, as was the tradition in Britain for a man of noble origin, but it bothered him, given the nonviolent practice of the group. So he one day asked Fox if it was OK for him to carry a sword, and it is said that Fox replied, "Carry it as long as you can."

No country has broken as many political treaties as the United States has. Of the over two hundred such treaties concluded with the Indian nations, every single one was broken. Hence the Indian nations were deeply suspicious of the settlers. The Quakers were the only Europeans who paid the Indians for the territories they occupied. Hence, when the Indians signed a treaty with the U.S. government, they often demanded that a Quaker be present at the signing of the treaty as a witness to its clauses.

At all times, Quakers have been at the forefront of protests and fights for numerous reforms: reforming prisons and psychiatric asylums, which were places of sheer horror at the end of the nineteenth century, and spearheading the fight against the Vietnam War and the invasion of Iraq. I myself worked for a Quaker NGO (nongovernmental organization) in Africa and can testify firsthand that I have never witnessed such respect of other cultures in a Western group. If there is any group I have met in my well over fifty-five years of professional involvement on four continents who live the statement "walk your talk," it is the Quakers.

KEY ASPECTS OF THE SPIRITUAL PATH

What follows are key aspects of the spiritual path to keep in mind on your journey to choose and maintain a spiritual practice.

Feeling Is the Basis for All Transformation

What frees one is not the intellectual or verbal definition of a truth but the feeling one has about it. The whole history of religion shows this. All authentic truth has to be lived on the level of the *heart,* not the mind. It is on the level of the heart that one finds the energy and motivation for change and where one finds love. It is the supreme spiritual quality par excellence. Transformation is a whole being, body-centered experience. A rather amazing folklore exists, describing the way a sudden spiritual understanding manifests itself through the body being seized by the spirit.

The Spiritual Path Is Not Always a Pleasant One

The more intensely committed the individual is, the greater the demand for an inner spiritual purification, which means the spiritual path is not always a path of roses. Some of the greatest saints and spiritual masters have had to walk through the most terrible inner hells and trials, even years of depression and existential despair.

In chapter 4 I will explain a particularly difficult period I endured, which I can only describe as a spiritual tsunami. During those difficult four years, I had, just in front of me, taped to my printer a sentence by Roger McGowen, a former death row inmate from Texas whose example has inspired (via his books, videos on YouTube, and website) hundreds of thousands around the globe: "I am suspended with my right hand by a rope, my left hand is tied behind my back, and someone is pulling at my feet, but I hang in there, and hang in and hang in" (Pradervand 2009). And he hung on for twenty-five years before an international defense committee I had organized managed to get him off death row (but not yet out of jail), where he had languished for a crime we are absolutely certain he did not commit. More is told about the story of Roger in the next chapter and in chapter 8, on the power of blessing.

In addition, I was often repeating a statement by an American metaphysician of the nineteenth century, Mary Baker Eddy, the remarkable founder of an American spiritual movement, Christian Science, which spread to many countries round the world but has almost disappeared today with the exception of a few countries. She wrote: "A deep sincerity is sure of success, for God takes care of it." And I knew I was totally sincere in my spiritual research. Even when I was in the deepest recesses of the valley of the shadow of death, I never ever doubted my sincerity, and this was a determining factor that enabled me to hang on—till the final liberation.

Mariana Caplan gives the example of Zen Roshi who, despite a most impressive spiritual career (which was certainly not so in my case), had a serious inner meltdown. After thirty years of meditation and having established Buddhist centers around the whole world, he broke down completely when his wife left him.

The spiritual path is anything but the guarantee of a prolonged sojourn in a spiritual Club Med! Maybe it offers only adventure (especially in the unsettled times we are experiencing), even if the final destination is assured sooner or later—and for all.

But It Can Be a Path of Overflowing Joy

If I mentioned the challenges one encounters on the spiritual path, it is because in our society of instant gratification, where people want "everything straight away," one certainly finds workshops of the following kind: "Spirituality in three weekends" in some beautiful resort—which isn't exactly the place to prepare you for the challenges of the spiritual way. But one has to insist that it can also be a path of overflowing joy, deep happiness, and fulfillment. I will never in my whole existence ever forget my encounter in Burkina Faso (West Africa) with a very simple man and devout follower of a spiritual path. His whole face was just a geyser of joy. He was the incarnation of overflowing happiness. Over thirty years later I still see his radiant features as if it were yesterday.

While the spiritual literature has its suffering saints, it also has many opposite examples like Brother Lawrence, a cobbler and cook in his monastery who transformed his kitchen into a place of radiant joy where, hour after hour, he lived the divine presence (Lawrence [1895] 2016).

One Infinite, Universal Mind

In these present times, when we are all becoming ever more acutely conscious of the total interdependence of the world, not only on the material, ecological, social, economic, and other planes, but also on the mental level, the idea of one Infinite Mind that links us all is more and more gaining ground. We can no longer live our spirituality in the closed container of our personal spiritual aspirations or in small spiritual groups or movements navigating in the wake of a spiritual teacher or self-proclaimed guru. We have to live our spirituality in relation to all others, for as all nondualist spiritual teachings show, we are already all one. Maybe one day a reader of this book will found the first spiritual movement akin to Avaaz—the nonprofit that promotes global activism.

Avoid Equating Religion with Spirituality

This distinction is very important. One can be a "highly religious" person and not have an ounce of spirituality, just as one can be an agnostic and manifest authentic spirituality in all one's behavior. This is especially true if one refers to Ellerby, who describes spirituality as our relationship to what we consider the most sacred in our lives; *sacred* here refers to what has the most meaning and value in our lives and merits our deepest reverence. He continues by describing what best expresses meaning, identity, and connection for us—realities that we live day by day. In that sense, we simply cannot avoid this dimension of life, be one a priest or an atheist, for such values determine the totality of our choices.

Religion on the other hand refers to a series of beliefs and sacred messages transmitted by some authority, which could be directly from God or a messenger of God. The origin of religions is lost in prehistory. They initially played an indispensable role in providing a structure of very basic ethical rules to societies totally devoid of such rules. An example of this is the role Moses and the Ten Commandments played in transforming an unruly group of former slaves into one of the great civilizing forces of the Middle East. In such societies, similar sets of rules or the Golden Rule ("Do unto your neighbor as you would want him to do to you," which exists in the ten major religions of the planet) represented a huge forward leap on the ethical level and also a protection against abuses in societies that were likely devoid of the very concept of human rights as currently under-stood and accepted in modern societies.

For me, one of the most powerful spiritual texts of human-ity I have ever come across is the famous definition of an authentic fast by the Hebrew prophet Isaiah. Compared to these lines, *The Communist Manifesto* of Karl Marx (for which I have the greatest respect) reads like a bedside book for retired Swiss bankers.

Here is this amazing text from chapter 58 of the Book of Isaiah in the Old Testament:

> *Is not this what I require of you as a fast:*
> *to loosen the fetters of injustice,*
> *to untie the knots of the yoke,*
> *to snap every yoke*
> *and set free those who have been crushed?*
> *Is it not sharing your food with the hungry,*
> *taking the homeless poor into your house,*
> *clothing the naked when you meet them,*
> *and never evading a duty to your kinsfolk?*
> *Then shall your light break forth as the dawn,*
> *and soon you will grow healthy like a wound*
> *   newly healed.*

What is amazing in this text is that the prophet makes *our* own healing and well-being depend on the healing and well-being of our neighbor and the world. There is no private paradise for Isaiah. Here, he gives one of the most fundamental spiritual messages of any authentic spirituality, which is that in today's world, we necessarily have to look for win-win solutions that work for all in all areas (the environment included), as all win-lose solutions (such as the relationship between the Global North and the Global South or between the wealthiest 1 percent, who pay little or no income tax, and the 99 percent, who have difficulty meeting basic needs) will end in a catastrophe for all. In a world where in 2020 the European cow received $2.00 per day in subsidies—which is more than the $1.90 per day that 700 million people worldwide live on, the World Bank's international line for extreme poverty—we cannot live our spirituality without taking such factors into account. In other words, these figures tell us one European cow is worth more to us than a poor human in the Third World.

Another very powerful message of the great religious teachings and spiritualities is that there exists another invisible world, which may be the "real" one, and that life does not end with the physical death of the body.

However, religions have also often played a very negative role, and the three great Abrahamic religions—Judaism, but more so Islam and especially Christianity—have been the source of some of the greatest massacres in world history. Pope Alexander V issued in the fifteenth century a papal bull or decree authorizing the Spanish and Portuguese to conquer the Americas and its native peoples, and Pope Nicolas V issued Romanus Pontifex authorizing the Portuguese to, among other things, enslave Africans. All of this done in the name of a gospel of unconditional love and nonviolence!

Like his predecessor Buddha, the basis of Jesus's teaching was spirituality *lived* in everyday life and in the affirmation of the apostle John: "He who lives love comes to the truth." This is possibly one of the most revolutionary affirmations made about spiritual truth. This is the message of Jesus and not a "correct" theology, as incarnated, for example, by the reformer Calvin. In the name of one who incarnated love as few, if any, of the great teachers of humanity did, Christian theologians have for centuries had unending quarrels on the exact meaning of Jesus's words and have assisted passively in the massacre of tens of millions.

Most religions also decreed forms of behavior that their members had to adhere to, and it is not rare that, especially in the past, such rules and regulations imprisoned their members in forms of behavior that ranged from the most absurd to the most sacred. Once more, this is especially true of the three religions of the word. In the case of Christianity, the book by the great French thinker and writer Jacques Ellul, *The Subversion of Christianity,* is, as mentioned earlier, a must-read for anyone who would understand how the clearly nondualist, freeing, and nonviolent message of one of the greatest avatars of human history was put on its head and carefully chloroformed by its own representatives. One can add that in the Christian world, over two thousand different teachings developed over time, teachings that divided rather than united believers, and Islam as well as Hinduism generated more than two hundred movements, which created divisions rather than bringing believers closer together.

Religions are still useful for many, but today, at least in the West, the great majority of spiritual seekers seem to be detaching themselves more and more from organized movements and churches.

2

Qualities to Foster for an Authentic Spiritual Search

THE FUNDAMENTAL SPIRITUAL PRECONDITION is to become your own authority. This issue is extremely important, for you always have the choice between either (a) submitting to some exterior spiritual authority, be it a spiritual teacher or guru, a confessor, a rigid teaching, a formal practice, a family tradition, or the pressure of a group (e.g., Mormons or Jehovah's Witnesses), or (b) adopting what you feel is best for you.

Absolutely no one outside of you can know your real needs at this level. In other words, either you accept the wine that is offered you (possibly diluting it somewhat) or you choose a wine that is really to your taste. This is also true in many other areas of our existence, such as health, nutrition, employment, a fundamental orientation in life, and many others. I went through this, giving up a very rigid spiritual path after close to forty years. It was most challenging and at times very unsettling.

Not everyone can undertake a spiritual path; it takes great determination. But it is possible.

Q *In which areas of my life am I really my own authority?*

If one refers to the text on integrity at the beginning of this book, even when faced with the teachings of the greatest spiritual teachers or the most sacred spiritual texts, such as the Hindu Bhagavad Gita, the Qur'an, the Buddhist Lotus Sutra, the Tao Te Ching (considered by many as the greatest sacred book ever written), the Bible, you still have to decide whether you accept their teachings and authority or not. To take the best known of these books in the West, the Bible, the Old Testament often attributes to God opinions that are very clearly human. In the books Leviticus and Deuteronomy, one can find punishments that are incredibly harsh, even outright cruel—and these are supposedly prescribed by a being who, in other texts of the same book, is presented as total, unconditional love. Is there the slightest coherence in such contradictions? One also finds verses that contradict each other completely side by side.

Thus, to determine your own viewpoint, you may need to seek out information from various books, experts of all sorts, and sometimes friends or acquaintances with a significant practice of the spiritual path, and from that mass of opinions you will need to define your own. This, however, is something we are all constantly doing in many walks of life—and we all know how challenging this can be. Concerning the treatments for cancer or Alzheimer's or other diseases, for instance, the mass of sometimes contradictory opinions can be disturbing, and you will often be led to follow your intuition. And do not believe science can offer the solution, for as the great Swiss pharmacologist Jean-Claude Etter was in the habit of saying in the last century, "in science, the truth of today is tomorrow's error." All the history of science proves this.

A very close friend of mine started having bladder problems. His brother recommended his own urologist, who prescribed radical chemotherapy and radiation therapy as the only solution, and woe to my friend if he did not follow these recommendations. He went to see another urologist who prescribed a mild treatment of quarterly injections, and the positive results were immediate.

Each one of us needs to find our own path to becoming our own authority. It is often an arduous path, and all will not manage to tread it. Personally, since I have really understood the deeper significance of my experience of love on the airplane I shared earlier, everything has become very simple for me: love has become my universal reference for absolutely everything, and I have since then been blessed with a serenity and equanimity that simply never leave me—and life has become so much simpler.

QUALITIES NECESSARY FOR
THE SPIRITUAL PATH

Let us now mention a few specific qualities needed to really progress on the spiritual path.

A Strong Intention

Absolutely nothing in life can be achieved without a clear, strong intention, and the clearer and firmer the intention, the greater the chances of success. From morning to night, we are governed by the intention of achieving something— which may be just a restful day or even the intention of doing nothing. Even that needs an intention! But those who achieve something exceptional often have a sort of master intention that governs their entire life, for example Queen Cleopatra of Egypt; Julian of Norwich, a medieval British nun we are just rediscovering who wrote some of the most deeply inspired texts on God's love in our possession; or Marie Curie, the French woman researcher and the only woman to have twice received the Nobel Prize.

In his book *Inevitable Grace,* to stress the importance of intention on the spiritual path, author Piero Ferrucci tells a both humorous and powerful story from India. A disciple comes to his guru and with an air of supplication asks him: "O Master, I so intensely desire to become enlightened. What do I need to do?" His master looks at him with both tenderness and skepticism and replies: "Come down to the river with me." The disciple, already imagining some secret initiation, follows his guru. They arrive at the river, which flows peace-fully close to the ashram. The master tells his disciple to bend forward with his head over the river. The master then seizes his disciple's head, pushes it under the water, and holds it there firmly. After a brief moment without breathing, the disciple starts struggling to free himself and finally manages to get away from the teacher's firm grip. Spouting water from all ori-fices, he looks at his master with an air of total bewilderment and disbelief. "The day you want enlightenment as intensely as you wanted to breathe, you will get it" is the master's terse comment.

A Sincere Motive

Joel S. Goldsmith (1892–1964), a great American mystic of the past century, has been for years now a precious guide on my spiritual path. Eckhart Tolle has said of him: "Joel Goldsmith was one of the great spiritual teachers of the twentieth century. His inspired books represent a vital contribution to the spiri-tual awakening of humanity." The spiritual path he taught is called The Infinite Way.

Related to the theme of this book, he wrote a deeply reassuring and comforting—but also provocative—text that addresses all sincere spiritual seekers (Goldsmith [1970] 2002).

> It makes no difference if we take the wrong path, we will end up where we belong if our motive is right. We need not be concerned whether the particular message we are follow-ing is the highest or the best. Our concern should be with

our motive. If that motive is to know God, then we can be in any teaching or no teaching and still be assured that we are going to end up knowing God aright, because the ripener of our soul is our desire or motive. When the heart cries out to know God, to tabernacle and commune with God, when the heart pushes us forward, compels us to read, listen, or study, when something within is driving us, be assured we are ripening, even though, at the moment, our outer experience does not bear testimony to it.

We go through years of suffering, either in illness, in lack, or in actual sin, and then, "in such an hour as ye think not the Son of man cometh," and we are awake. In every case where I have seen this happen, the answer has been the same. Deep down there was a longing to know God aright, to know truth, a longing to find the nature of "My kingdom," or the nature of "My peace," and as we continue in our study and meditation, regardless of whether we feel spiritual or not, the ripening process is going on.

At a very deep level there must be a desire to know God correctly, to know truth, a deep aspiration to discover the nature of the Kingdom of God. (This mythical expression simply means an inner state of peace, plenitude, and joy nothing can destroy.)

In other words, what Joel is telling us is that the sincerity of our motive and intention carries us as nothing else can. This is so well expressed in a favorite spiritual story of mine taken from the wonderful book of stories *Au bord du Gange* by Martine Quentric-Séguy. Quentric-Séguy narrates the tale of the seeker Mohan, who becomes a spiritual teacher, and Saralah, his disciple.

Disciple

For some time, Mohan wandered the roads of India in search of a spiritual teacher. One day, he finally finds such a master with whom he stays, caring for his master's cows during the day, studying at his feet in the evening. At the death of his master, who had a phenomenal knowledge and grasp of the holy writings of Hinduism, Mohan hit the road once more.

One day, completely famished and exhausted, he reaches a poor village whose inhabitants get him back into decent shape. Discovering his rare knowledge of the scriptures and Vedanta, they offer him permanent hospitality, as they have no Brahmin in the village.

Little by little, a small circle of disciples from the village and the surrounding areas builds up around Mohan. Among the young men following Mohan's teachings is a teenager called Saralah, who is absolutely convinced that Mohan is the best teacher he could ever find, and who would give him the sacred mantra that would enable him to reach illumination. Mohan, however, has a very poor opinion of Saralah's spiritual capacities.

Unbeknown to his teacher, Saralah sleeps on Mohan's doorstep, should the master ever express some need even at night. One night, pressed by a natural need, Mohan trips over Saralah's body.

His angry reaction is to bellow: "Always you!" And point-
ing to the road leading out of the village, he shouts: "Leave
immediately and don't return before I call for you!"

However, Saralah interprets "Always You" as his holy
mantra, You being the Divine. Wherever he is, whomever or
whatever he meets—a peasant on his cart, a wild animal on a
jungle path, a terrible storm, hunger, or a good meal—his one
and only response to absolutely everything is to see a divine
manifestation: always "Always You." As year adds upon year,
there emanates from Saralah an amazing energy of deep serenity and contentment, of quiet joy, and an all-pervading love.

One day he reaches a village where a widow has lost her
only son. In the past in India, the situation of widows was
very difficult, and for a poor widow to lose her only son was
a major tragedy, a real cataclysm. When Saralah arrives, the
villagers are preparing to cremate the body and are running
to and fro to chase evil spirits and prevent the spirit of the
deceased from returning to his body. They are afraid the boy's
spirit will not leave and will turn into a phantom and haunt
the village. The villagers, sensing the profoundly spiritual
nature of Saralah, beg him to pray for the deceased, while the
bereft mother implores him to save her son.

Saralah explains that he has not the gift of appeasing the
souls of the deceased nor of awakening them. "But I will repeat
the powerful mantra my master Mohan taught me." And he
settles down at the foot of the pyre and plunges totally into
the holy name.

And suddenly the young man sits up, astonished to find

himself on a pyre, and climbs down. The stunned villagers start bringing small gifts to Saralah, which they lay at his feet. However, the latter refuses the slightest acknowledgment. "It is not to me that you must make these gifts, it is to my teacher Mohan."

Without realizing it, Saralah has traveled a huge circle of thousands of miles and has come within a short distance of Mohan's village, where he still teaches and is fairly well known in the region.

Soon after, a large crowd of people comes to tell Mohan the unbelievable story of this resurrection brought about by one of his students. But Mohan knows that not a single one of his students is capable of performing such a miracle, not to mention himself. So he asks the name of the student, and people in the crowd reply "Saralah." Totally stunned, Mohan asks them to tell Saralah that his teacher is calling for him.

Rapidly, the villagers catch up with Saralah, who in the meantime had left the village. "Your master Mohan asks you to come and see him in his village." For Saralah, this is *the* great day, the day he had almost stopped hoping for, when his teacher would call him back.

When he arrives at Mohan's modest home, he falls at his feet. Gently, Mohan raises him up and asks him what his mantra is and when he received it. Saralah narrates his version of the incident: "And then you gently rested your foot on me as I lay on the doorstep and said: "Always You.""

And suddenly, the whole scene comes back to Mohan. He remembers his profound irritation at discovering Saralah's presence on his doorstep, hears himself yell "Always you!" and order Saralah to leave the village and never return until he, Mohan, calls him back. He sees Saralah's radiant features, feels the quiet strength and inner light that his whole being emanates compared to the old, completely desiccated and parched teacher he has become, lost on the path of his sterile intelligence, replete with a theoretical knowledge expressed in formulas and wise quotes, all in the head, nothing in the heart.

In a once-in-a-lifetime moment of deep humility, Mohan falls at the feet of Saralah and begs him: "O Master, teach me."

Perseverance

This quality is a prerequisite of any meaningful achievement, whatever it may be, and the spiritual path is certainly no exception. The British philosopher and statesman of the late sixteenth and early seventeenth centuries Francis Bacon (1561–1626) already stated that "in all undertaking, perseverance is the key to success."

And the American author H. Jackson Brown Jr. observed that when faced with rocks, the stream will always get the upper hand, not with force but with perseverance. The rock on the spiritual path represents the ego—and I will come back to this issue further.

A wonderful example of perseverance is the discovery of the electric bulb by Thomas Edison, the fourth-most prolific inventor in human history (he patented 1,093 inventions in the United States alone). He failed around ten thousand times before discovering the wire covered with carbon, which formed the basis of the first electric bulbs, certainly one of the great inventions in human history.

All society was aware of his research to find a conduit for electricity capable of producing artificial light. One day, after he had experienced already five thousand failures, a young journalist came to interview him. "Mr. Edison, how does it feel to have failed already five thousand times?"

It is said that Edison straightened up to his maximum height and replied, "Young man, I have not failed five thousand times. I have gotten five thousand times closer to the solution that will finally work."

You may be lamenting your incessant (but apparently unsuccessful) attempts to overcome your ego. "Join the club" as the saying goes. You may continue your efforts as long and as often as you wish (and the bonus is that these efforts are free of charge!). If after ten thousand trials or ten years of effort you have advanced a few feet (figuratively speaking), congratulate yourself. You are on the right path. Perseverance is an indispensable quality for anyone on the spiritual path. It is the radical opposite of the mantra of the consumer society: "I want everything, immediately." Recently I saw on the train a young man wearing a T-shirt with the inscription: "An abundance of everything is not enough."

Saint Teresa: A Great Spiritual Seer
Who Encouraged Perseverance

Saint Teresa was unquestionably one of the great figures of medieval spirituality. In the book Megan Don devoted to her,

Don writes that Teresa reminds us that "it is easy to become lured into spiritual sensationalism, that is, expecting to have experiences that make us feel especially connected to the Beloved" (Don 2011).

While we pray and meditate, we may see, hear, or feel the divine presence in many ways. However, it is also possible, and often very likely, that we will not experience the Divine in any form. The soul may feel, as a result of this lack of experience, that it is not making the desired connection and therefore that something is wrong. We can then become overly concerned about the nature of spiritual experience and seek ways to further enhance spiritual pleasure rather than simply allowing the spirit of the Beloved to guide us. In her book, Don wrote that Teresa believed "these times of 'dryness' are given to us by the Beloved so that we may become more spiritually mature."

> Just as a baby first crawls and then gradually learns to walk, so too must we learn to take our own first spiritual steps. But we must also note that they may not always be in the direction that we would like to take, and we may not always agree with the Beloved's methods. As we are walking in this unwelcome dryness, we may witness others being given all sorts of spiritual gifts. Teresa says we are to "blindfold the eyes of the mind" (*TL*, 81) so as not to compare our journey with theirs. And she asked what difference it should make to us what others are or are not receiving. Who are we to question the workings of the Beloved and of other souls?

Under no circumstances, said Teresa, are we to give up our time of prayer and meditation, no matter how tedious it becomes; this would be like saying that since we are no longer receiving anything, we will not spend our time this way. Can you imagine acting like this with our friends and lovers? What if, in a moment of not receiving anything from them, we ceased spending time with them? The small amount of time we do spend in prayer and meditation, Teresa believed, should be given wholly to the Beloved: we should consider it not ours but the Beloved's. And we should become determined never to take it back—not for any trial or challenge we experience, not for any contradiction in our life, not for any dryness we experience in prayer. Ultimately, what Teresa is saying is that no matter what is occurring in our life, we are not to abandon the relationship that is the very core of our existence.

Living with the Beloved does not always mean being bathed in delight and tenderness (even though this is what we would all prefer). What it does mean is serving the divine relationship with fortitude and humility. When things in our life become less than pleasurable, naturally we want them to become easier. Teresa ascertained, however, that such a desire lacks the freedom our spirit requires. The spirit needs to roam where it is guided, and we can join in this courageous adventure by allowing it to accomplish what it is here to do. (Don 2011)

I have already said that the spiritual path is not a path of roses, and I wish to come back to this issue because without strong perseverance it will be very difficult to go through the stretches of desert that await many spiritual seekers. These barren stretches do not await all, and there are certainly some spiritually advanced persons whose progress was mostly achieved by walking through green pastures. But in the increasingly agitated and challenging world we live in, this will certainly not become the norm, and by far.

Roger McGowen: A Remarkable Example of Perseverance

A person who had to manifest a quite exceptional endurance and perseverance is my friend Roger McGowen, twenty-five years on Texas death row (a place that is the incarnation of hell to the power of ten) for a crime that we have the absolute certitude he did not commit. (In the meantime, we got him off death row, though he is still in prison.) But if you are poor and black, your chances of getting fair justice in Texas are really slim. He had an alcoholic lawyer who did not even visit Roger before the trial, prepared Roger's defense on the basis of the police report condemning him, used to brag that he was the American lawyer who had had the most clients condemned to death (seventeen), and fell asleep snoring loudly during the trial of his client! He used to sometimes meet with the judge and the state attorney for a drink before the trial. Little surprise that later the Texas Bar Association withdrew his right to defend death row inmates—but the harm was already done.

Roger understandably entered death row in a state of deep revolt and anger. But one day he awoke to the fact that he was condemning himself to a sour future, so intense did the psychosomatic symptoms due to his anger become. He then realized that he could only count on himself. So, alone in hell, he started searching for his own spiritual path, his own approach to facing his plight. He entered death row in 1987 and had already been there ten years when we started corresponding (1997). After a few years, his letters struck me as so amazing I decided to publish them, first in French and later on in English.*

The response to his first book in French was just amazing. People spontaneously started sending funds for his defense— one woman who had just received an inheritance sent in over $50,000. For hundreds of people, myself included, Roger has become a real master and spiritual guide. Thanks to the generosity of readers everywhere—including some elderly on tiny pensions who sent in $15 with little notes saying, for example, "It's the best I can do, but I do it with joy"—we were able to hire a good lawyer who got him off death row but not out of prison. He is presently in a prison of over two thousand inmates, which he is transforming profoundly, solely by his presence. Three NGOs have been set up in Europe just for his defense. Nicolas Pallay, one of the most talented journalists

---

*Pradervand, *Messages of Life from Death Row*. The French edition has Roger as the main author, but our U.S. lawyer feared that if this were the case in English, the Texas authorities would seize the proceeds of the sales, so it was published under my name.

of the best Swiss TV show, made a remarkable one-hour film on Roger, including interviews of Roger on death row.

Roger offers an extraordinary encouragement for anyone who feels alone on their spiritual path, for here is a person lost in one of the worst hells of this planet, with not a single person, not one single book to guide him (not even the faintest trace of a chaplain on death row), who, like a mountain climber facing a steep rock face, little by little finds his spiritual path.

A Total Consecration

The spiritual path is certainly not designed for dabblers or amateurs, even enlightened ones. It is essential that your spiritual search be a top priority in your life—for many it will be *the* top priority. You will reap exactly what you sow—in efforts, in time, and, above all, in love, for this is the basic law of the universe.

One of the loveliest illustrations of this consecration is given to us in one of those savory tales of which Tolstoy was such a master.

The Three Hermits

A Russian bishop newly nominated to his bishopric bordering the Black Sea decides to visit the different communities of his diocese by ship. As the ship approaches a small island, the numerous pilgrims on the ship all congregate on the side nearest the island. The bishop asks why they are engaging in this curious behavior. He is told the island is inhabited by three hermits who pray all day long, and the pilgrims hope to catch a glimpse of them.

The bishop asks the captain if he could stop the ship at the island so that he could go and visit the hermits. In imperial Russia, the request of a bishop was close to an order, so the captain drops anchor, and the bishop sets off for the island in a small rowboat with two sailors. As the boat gets closer to the island, the bishop sees three old men with very long beards awaiting him on the shore.

Once he has landed, the bishop explains who he is and asks the three hermits how they pray. They reply: "You are three, we are three, have mercy on us." The bishop replies that they have great merit and seem to have understood something about the Holy Trinity, but he also tells them that they are not praying correctly.

He proceeds to teach them the Lord's Prayer. But these three simple souls are not great intellectuals and even memorizing something relatively short is a superhuman challenge for them. The bishop makes them repeat the prayer time and again. Finally, by late afternoon, the hermits seem to have mastered the prayer. So the bishop returns to the ship.

In the evening, as he cannot sleep, he joins the helmsman. Suddenly, the latter utters a loud cry and crosses himself three times: a shining light is approaching the ship, and the bishop then discerns the three hermits gliding over the water to catch up with them. When they reach the ship, they shout to the stunned bishop: "Oh Father, we have forgotten the correct way of praying to have our prayers answered." All the bewildered bishop can reply is: "Holy men, I have nothing to teach you. Pray for us poor sinners," And the three hermits return to their island, gliding across the water. A bright light is visible on the horizon till morning.

In the spiritual literature one finds many such stories and examples that underscore the importance of *total* consecration in the pursuit of a spiritual goal.

What is wonderful in Tolstoy's story is that though the hermits' prayer seems totally incorrect on the level of form, even slightly ridiculous, they achieved their aim, illustrating perfectly an already quoted statement of Joel Goldsmith. In Christianity's long history and its search for "correct" definitions of a truth or "correct" ways of behaving, the religion managed so often to get bogged down in incredible theological debates, and these, alas, even led to wars and massacres.

For me, the number one reason of our temporary sojourn on Earth is simply to grow in love. "Simply," yes! But *what* a challenge. However, as long as we keep this aim clearly in mind—and especially in our hearts!—whatever mistakes we make, whatever detours we take, the universe, the Source will always lead us back to the right path. Remember, we are never, never alone on this path, even if experiences like that of Mother Teresa would lead some to believe the contrary, as we will see in chapter 4. An Infinite Intelligence, which is *only love,* watches over *every single one* of our steps. We need to really *feel* this, not only know it. It is such an unbelievable reassurance for anyone on the spiritual path.

Discernment

I repeat the statement of Byron Katie who said that confusion is the most marked characteristic of this world. In practically all fields, including the scientific domain, one discovers the most contradictory opinions. For instance, take a recent example that touches most of us: COVID-19. Be it the wearing of masks, the mode of transmission of the disease, the efficacy of confinement, its origin and treatment, you will find, even among eminent experts, a multitude of opinions, sometimes totally contradictory.

In the field of food consumption, take a well-known institute in Florida that proposes diets without any sugar whatsoever (hence no fruit) and no salt, essentially based on sprouted seeds and seaweed, which of course banishes alcohol and coffee as poisonous, not to mention umpteen other restrictions. However, your family doctor (who knows almost nothing of nutrition, which is, alas, still the case of many doctors) recommends a glass of wine in the evening and, being a coffee addict, does not say a word of coffee's potentially deleterious impact. Thus, you and I are obliged to navigate among a near infinity of contradictory opinions, including opinions from Internet sites, the value of which we are nearly totally incapable of evaluating. We are constantly faced in so many areas with a distressing variety of opinions.

In the spiritual field, we are hardly better off. Between your Evangelical cousin who warns you that unless you acknowledge

Jesus Christ as your personal savior you will go straight to hell or the crazy jihadists who arrive in a village and massacre all its inhabitants because they do not belong to their branch of Islam or the author of these lines (who in the prehistory of his life studied theology) who will tell you the only really important thing is to grow in love and that all these theologies based on condemnation and fear are only the expression of unhandled inner fears—well, the differences are as great as in the field of nutrition.

The needed discernment will certainly come to you if you follow the basic rules of the text on integrity, which you will find in chapter 1. Your personal integrity, that is, your ability to be really yourself, constitutes a guide that I believe is infallible. Does the teaching that is offered to you increase your joy? Does it deepen your peace, that "peace which passes all understanding" and all human explanations? Above all, does it give you wings to love more, to love unconditionally, to welcome any human being—however hostile, extreme, sick, aggressive that person may be as your sister or brother? These are fundamental questions to ask yourself and to which it is essential you find a reply.

Always Stay Open

Unless one follows a spiritual teacher or a very rigorous spiritual path (which I did at one period in my life and it killed all my joy), the spiritual path can be very unpredictable. It is essential to stay open to what is unpredictable. Many years ago, this frightened me. Today, I welcome it with curiosity. For if a path becomes too predictable, it can be dangerous. Spiritual discipline and routine can become a way of simply seeking inner security. So give yourself occasional spiritual check-ups! I myself experienced this subtle deformation at one moment on my spiritual path, when the slightest break in my routine started to create an inner insecurity. My discipline had acquired a magical dimension, as if the discipline, in itself, guaranteed my security and not the spiritual truth it was supposed to transmit. In psychology, such forms of behavior are called magical, and many religions are often packed full of such practices.

Discipline

In our culture, which too often claims to offer "everything, immediately," *discipline* is a word that is not so popular with many of our contemporaries. Yet ask any renowned sportsman or woman, any musician with recognized talents, whether the path to competence and success was easy, and I doubt you will receive a convinced yes.

My closest friend was many years ago the best American talent in the field of flamenco, to the extent of receiving a standing ovation from a delirious crowd in Mexico City, a rare tribute for a "gringo." His life is the perfect illustration of this discipline. When fifteen, he discovered flamenco from a secondhand record his mother bought in a sale. That record transformed his life. He started training alone. Then he had the good fortune of meeting in New York one of the greatest masters of flamenco of the world at that time, Carlos Montoya, who offered him free flamenco lessons. He practiced at least ten hours a day. In the evening, he used to work in a restaurant to earn a living. He only slept a few hours per night. And he became one of the recognized masters of the day in the field of the flamenco guitar. However, the Edisons of sport or music do not exactly overpopulate the planet!

The same truth is valid in the case of spirituality. Growing numbers of people are turning toward spirituality as it can be a remarkable source of serenity in our troubled times, and even a small investment of time brings rapid returns. But between that and making it the number one priority of one's life and learning to make certain that every single thought is beholden or captive to love, there is a long, long way to travel, sometimes on rocky terrain.

We live in a paradoxical culture. On the one hand, never before in history have people worked so little to earn their living. One only has to read the unbelievable descriptions of working conditions in factories in the nineteenth and early twentieth centuries to realize how privileged we are. And yet there has never been a time in history when so many people complain that "I just don't have the time to do what I want or need to do" or "I'm always on the run" and similar statements. The explanation is very simple: there has never been a period in the existence of our societies when people had so many things and cultural or other opportunities (travel, etc.) to consume. And it is not improving, by any means, despite the pandemic. As a result, many people have great difficulty establishing clear priorities.

Because for most people, it's a question of priorities. If

you really wish to make spirituality one of the fundamental priorities of your life, you will sooner or later have to cut the time you spend on social networks, television, the Internet, and leisure activities. There are, of course, certain categories of people whose hours are crammed with often conflicting priorities. I am thinking of single working mothers working close to full-time, raising children, and doing all the household tasks. But even for such categories of people there exists what I call *unconventional spirituality,* that is, finding a kind of practice you can do as you work.

One luminous example is Brother Lawrence, already mentioned earlier on. He acquired long ago an international and especially interconfessional reputation. Lawrence transformed his kitchen into a place where he had nonstop conversations with God. His radiant spirituality turned him into a confessor for many sometimes renowned people, and he even became a friend of the great Fénelon, to whom the king entrusted his son's education. Not one word of theology in Lawrence's message but simply the felt Presence he radiated all around himself.

Whether you are a cashier, salesperson, or bus driver, you too can practice this kind of spirituality.

In the Heart, Not the Head

Joel Goldsmith, the great American mystic of the last century who founded a teaching he called The Infinite Way that he presents in a slim volume (he wrote around thirty books), was also an amazing healer. At one time in his life, he was daily receiving well over a hundred phone calls for help with various problems, and most were healed, some instantaneously.

He insists that truth has to be felt in the heart, not described intellectually. It is feeling the truth that heals, not its "correct" presentation. He explains that when he received a call for support, he immediately forgot the name of the patient and the problem! He plunged into the silence until he felt the presence of the Divine and the assurance that all was already in order, already healed. And the patient was nearly always healed.

In his book *The Art of Spiritual Healing*, Joel explains what happened once during a flu epidemic. He had seen patients at his office the whole morning. The preceding evening and during the morning, he had received thirty-five requests for help. At noon, when he looked at his agenda, he realized that for a full hour he had no more patients, which had never happened before. So he took the whole hour just to plunge into the silence and simply listen to and feel the Source. During the afternoon, almost all the thirty-five people for whom he had not done any specific spiritual work called to say they were healed. Joel explains that his thought had reached such a high level during that hour that as soon as the patients' thoughts "touched" his thought, they were healed.

To feel the truth, the Divine, is very powerful.

3

Spiritually
Transmitted Diseases

IN THE MEDICAL FIELD, STD signifies sexually transmitted diseases. In this book, the expression means spiritually transmitted diseases. And in the field of spirituality (as in the medical field), they are quite numerous and pernicious, as they have their own immune system while being sometimes very contagious. Any spiritual researcher or person traveling the spiritual path needs to be at least aware of their existence, for the spiritual antibiotics are of slightly more complex use than those applied in medicine. Here are a few of these STDs.

SPIRITUAL FAST FOOD

Our consumer society celebrates speed, multitasking, and instantaneous gratification in all areas. Therefore, it is not at all surprising that it attempts to appropriate also the field of spirituality—and manages very well! For instance, consider trainings that promise to turn you into an awakened person or shaman in a few weekends or a ten-day workshop. Before following a training you don't know much about, really inquire about the reputation of the course and the trainer, which might demand that you ask some indiscreet questions. This is your full right. Never embark on a training or weekend class without being certain that it is of real value and based on proven criteria.

PSEUDOSPIRITUALITY

This is a spirituality of imitation, like a person who wears a fake mink coat hoping others will believe it's the real thing. The people who practice this kind of spirituality have been to all the right trainings, have listened to fashionable gurus, and have read the latest books in the field of spirituality, but they are not ready to undertake the hard work necessary (especially today) to really progress on the spiritual path. They are constantly making statements like: "Ah, but it's his karma" or "She must have done something really serious in a previous incarnation"—when the fact is that we understand almost nothing about how the universe really functions and the spiritual laws governing reality. Personally, I feel I understand less and less of how "reality" functions—not more than 0.0000000000001 percent. I know just enough to fuel me every day on my chosen path, which is that I am here to learn how to love more. And I feel I am still in the kindergarten of my spiritual quest.

RIGID RULES

In some groups—such as certain extremely conservative Protestant Evangelicals, Jehovah's Witnesses, and numerous others, be they Christian, Muslim, or Jewish—there are subtle, frequently unspoken, agreements and rules on how to dress, speak, and behave that end up putting people on a rigid path. It's very reassuring for the members of the group but dangerous for any person who wishes to keep his or her identity. There is, of course, a deep psychological gratification in identifying with a group or a charismatic leader, but it can prove most harmful to one's sense of identity.

THE DELUSION THAT
YOUR PATH IS THE BEST

This is the idea that the group or the path to which one belongs is the most evolved, the most spiritual or advanced, that it's simply better than the others. This was the case with the spiritual path I embarked on for many years. It can easily lead to a subtle form of spiritual pride, which was certainly true in my case. In the movement to which I had adhered—and which was absolutely amazing in terms of spiritual healing, which is why I stayed with it for so long—there was a quasi-deification of its nineteenth-century founder. There is a great difference between acknowledging that one has found what turns out to be the best path *for oneself* and the best path, period.

THE BELIEF BASED ON A FEELING OF SEPARATION THAT YOUR EGO IS YOU

This is unquestionably the most frequent form of STD. It consists in identifying with one's ego, which was very useful while growing up, in affirming our personality as a child and a young adult, but which ends up running the whole show to the extent that people believe that the ego really is who they are.

Mariana Caplan has some very strong words on this theme. She writes:

> The fundamental misunderstanding of our own true identity, which is the core problem all spiritual seekers face, is the foundational base of all spiritually transmitted diseases. This unshakable conviction that "I am who I believe myself to be"—which tends to be equally strong among those who understand this concept intellectually and those who do not—is so virulent that it taints every aspect of our spiritual practice, from service to meditation to ritual. Most of us spend our entire lives on the path with this spiritual dis-ease embedded in our consciousness. It infects teachers, students, religious movements, and all spiritual traditions. (Caplan 2009)

I would add that it is certainly the most difficult STD to eradicate.

A modest personal approach, which provided me with the means to heal this challenge of the ego's dominance, is a very brief prayer that was given to me seven thousand feet up in a beautiful centennial chalet in the Swiss Alps and which I have been using for thirty years now:

Shine as me
and may I be so You
that all those I encounter may experience me as
Your radiant Presence, Your unconditional love
    and forgiveness.
May they no longer see me, but
Only, only, ONLY YOU.

This little prayer was the water of the torrent that eroded the rock of the ego—and continues to do so with measurable effects. Use it daily, even five, ten, or more times a day. Or better still, compose your own prayer. It is essential that it be uttered from the heart and as a deep aspiration of your whole being toward the ego's disappearance, which alone will transform you into a transparent channel for the Divine, the Source.

The Sufi poet Rumi from Persia can certainly be counted among the great spiritual writers of humanity. He wrote a remarkably beautiful text on the death of the ego, which distills in a few lines the basics of what needs to happen to expel this imposter from our home.

The Grapes of My Body Can Only Become Wine

The grapes of my body can only become wine
after the winegrower has trampled them.

I abandon my spirit as the grapes to his
    trampling,
that the heart of my heart can only become
    inflamed
and dance with joy.
Although the grapes continue to bleed blood and
    to sob:
"I can no longer support such anguish and such
    cruelty"
he who tramples them puts tear plugs in his ears:
"I do not work in ignorance.
You can deny me if you wish, you have all the
    excuses to do so.
But it is I who am the Master of this Work.
And when through my passion you reach
    Perfection,
You will never cease blessing my name."

If the spiritual path is undertaken with absolute sincerity, with a very clear intention and a deep fervor, it will sooner or later reach that state of a total dissolution of the ego (and for the majority this will probably not happen in their present incarnation). So beware. If you are not ready to dismantle the ego, do not follow the spiritual path, for inevitably there will be periods of stagnation and even regression, where the illusion of being somewhat illumined will completely disappear. There will be periods when one imagines that one has made decisive progress and then suddenly realizes how far there is still to go, that one is still only in grade school, maybe even in kindergarten. And one stands there, in one's nakedness, wondering what is really happening.

That is just the moment to rejoice—for only the little ego can feel sad or depressed, disappointed, discouraged, angry, and thus it unmasks itself. And you? You smile, remembering that the ego is not the real you! For your true selfhood is already one with the Divine, the Source—which some call God.

Q *How does the ego manifest itself in my existence?*

4

Spiritual Darkness

THE EXPRESSION *the dark night of the soul* refers to a spiritual crisis that can last for years, sometimes even among the greatest spiritual seekers. Mother Teresa wrote to her spiritual counsellor that: "Darkness is such that I really do not see—neither with my mind nor with my reason—the place of God is blank—There is no God in me—when the pain of longing is so great—I just long & long for God—and then it is that I feel—He doesn't want me—He is not there— . . . God doesn't want me—Sometimes—I just hear my own heart cry out—'My God' and nothing else comes—The torture and pain I can't explain" (Kolodiejchuk 2007).

That is how one of the greatest spiritual personalities of the contemporary world could feel.

Mother Teresa was canonized nineteen years after her death and was a modern icon for tens of millions of believers worldwide. If ever there was a saint revered by the public and by all faiths, it is she! Yet according to one of her biographers, the last fifty years of her life were a total spiritual desert.

For fifty years, she did not have the slightest feeling of the divine presence, with a brief exception of five weeks in 1959. She even spoke of her famous smile as a mask that hid her deep inner disarray and that led her to doubt the existence of heaven and even of God.

In her biography, she describes her inner state with words such as *dryness, obscurity, solitude,* and *torture* and even compares her experience to hell. There were moments when she couldn't even pray. And she even came to describe her soul as a "block of ice."

As I mentioned on page 17, I myself went through a period on my spiritual path when a tsunami blew away my whole existence—and I really mean absolutely everything! I had been for close to forty years on a spiritual path that its promoters described as the ultimate, the *nec plus ultra* of all spiritual paths, and the highest spiritual truth around. I even looked with some condescension upon those on "less advanced" paths than mine. I used to spend hours each day in spiritual study—but it was all in the head. And then, quite literally, my *whole* life fell apart. I mean it—just everything. First, my marriage, which so many people gave as an example of the ideal couple, fell apart, and I moved out of the family apartment.

Then my health cratered. I, who practically never consulted a doctor, was diagnosed with a serious ailment, which supposedly necessitated the heaviest treatments available. My energy fell through the floor, and I was unable to conduct my workshops, which were my main source of income. Last but not least, my spiritual path of forty years exploded to smithereens. One or two of those challenges would have been enough but all five at the same time—I'll let you choose your own adjective for my predicament. You could have picked up the small pieces of what was left of me with a teaspoon.

And it lasted close to four years. Four years of hell, of radically questioning myself, even entertaining suicidal thoughts.

This was me, the great trainer and writer? The person people used to put on a pedestal? Who had published books with titles like *No Longer a Victim* and *Happiness Can Be Learned*?

Yes—the same fellow!

Then one day, grace—that magical tool of providence—intervened, and I once again started climbing. And today everything is far better than before, and I can really say: *thank you, thank you, thank you* for that passage through the Valley of Baca, the valley of tears, a purgatory that helped clear me of so many old spiritual and other relics I had carefully cloistered deep down in my spiritual garden. Now I have the deepest conviction that all challenges help us progress on our life path, as long as we are totally sincere in our approach and manifest an unrelenting perseverance.

Sometimes, as Mariana Caplan explains, the basis of this crisis is the awareness that one had built a personality that was not a reflection of what we truly are. This dark night of the soul can even include, as in the case of Mother Teresa, periods of complete and total loss of contact with the Source, the aim of which is often to burn the residues of the ego and to annihilate the remaining obstacles preventing our ultimate union with this Source.

The trials of Mother Teresa contain two fundamental lessons for us:

1. If she was able to cross such a spiritual desert for fifty years, then maybe we will manage to cross deserts of lesser duration without falling to pieces.
2. It seems that what enabled her to persevere was above all the power of her intention and her spirit of service. It was much more important for her to hold in her arms a dying beggar on a Calcutta street than to enjoy spiritual rapture—or even feel normally well.

But once more, if we believe the universe is a place of immense benevolence and that, notwithstanding appearances to the contrary, it is leading us all to the goal of complete fullness of being, we will be able to traverse such inner hells with less suffering. In my valley of tears, of Baca, two statements by Mary Baker Eddy were of immense support to me: "Trials are proofs of God's (Love's) care" and "There is not one redundant drop in the cup of your trials." Not one drop! That's quite a statement—and of course, this was based on her own existence and trials, of which she certainly had her fair share. Now one of my favorite mantras is: "All is a gift"—a bit like the "Always You" in the story of Mohan and Saralah told in chapter 2.

One of the most intense and universal strivings of human beings (and the animal kingdom, too) is for security at all costs. In our modern societies, this is manifested in the innumerable forms of insurance covering almost everything, the search for physical security in practically all fields of existence via the most sophisticated systems imaginable (and new ones are constantly being invented), numerous forms of old age insurance, the search for medicines that will heal every disease, numerous systems to compensate the unemployed—the list is endless. Not to mention our personal search for security in our human relationships.

Yet, on the level of our societies, everything is constantly changing in our lives. We will be greatly helped if we manage to integrate the Buddhist concept of impermanence. Nothing appears permanent, nothing is fixed once and for all. A Buddhist teacher from Bhutan, Dzongsar Khyentse, writes: "The absence of fear is generated when you can learn to appreciate incertitude." One could even add rejoice in it! Buddhism stresses that the only permanent thing in our lives *is* change! So drop this hunt for security at all costs. It can exist solely on a spiritual level, and even then, only in a nondual approach as in some forms of Advaita Vedanta or, in the Christian field, a thinker like Joel Goldsmith, where there is no longer the slightest sense of separation from God. But that theme in itself would be another book!

5

Living the Nondual Life

TWO PRECIOUS, CRUCIAL TOOLS will help guide you and keep you on your spiritual path and living the nondual life: nonrejection, or saying yes to everything in your life, and nonpossession.

THE GREAT YES TO LIFE

A very important practice taught by various nondual approaches like that of the contemporary French teacher Arnaud Desjardins, the great popularizer of Buddhism and the tantric teachings from Kashmir, is the practice of nonrejection, in other words the acceptance of absolutely everything that happens in our life, as illustrated in the story of Saralah. This could even become your spiritual path. This path is not so much a specific practice or movement with teachings you must follow but a manner of being and responding to life, a practice you develop on your own.

One of the basic dimensions of Tantrism or the practice

of nonrejection consists in facing any situation, whatever it may be, in a productive and positive manner, which enables us to avoid excluding any experience in life. Or as Arnaud Desjardins writes: "If you wish to know the silence, take a great interest in noise." One of the main teachings of Desjardins was to say *yes* to all aspects of life, an idea I expand on in my book *Le grand oui à la vie* (*The Great Yes to Life,* not yet published in English).

As we learn to say yes to absolutely everything, to open up to and master what before disturbed us or that we rejected, these same things lose all power over us (e.g., loud traffic noise, the way your son or daughter dresses, a terribly rude waiter, the bad behavior of politicians). In his book *L'audace de vivre* Desjardins writes: "Once the ego no longer finds an adversary, then the ego no longer exists. Since its birth, what characterizes the ego is being against. . . . That's why the word YES is the absolute weapon against the ego."

Mariana Caplan very rightly stresses that where you have two, you have duality in one form or another, which implies two sides in our consciousness. But when we say yes to our entire experience, the duality inherent in our resistance to ourselves and our life disappears in a unity born of a complete acceptance of our life and our experiences as they occur. In other words, as she explains, we then cease trying to force our life into preconceived molds and learn to accept it exactly as it is. She adds that when we learn by attention, practice, study, courage, and an immense perseverance (the role of which I have already stressed) to say yes to all that is, however undesirable it may seem, the whole of life becomes a fascinating experience.

I myself had a rather rare experience that stressed the power of saying yes to absolutely everything, including something that appeared as a totally undeserved misfortune. At the beginning of the eighties, I lived in one of the most beautiful places in Switzerland, on a little mountain called Le Mont Pélerin just above the city of Vevey. I had a breathtaking view of Lake Geneva and the Alps beyond, small sweet-scented pine forests to do my jogging with the neighbor's friendly dog following me, and a small grocery store that opened at 6:30 a.m. only six hundred feet from my apartment.

One day, I left my little paradise and moved into an apartment on one of the noisiest, most polluted streets of Geneva. Jogging on that street in dirty slushy snow in winter was not my dream, so I purchased one of those home exercise bicycles. I threw myself into this new exercise with my customary enthusiasm, but after a few weeks I manifested clear signs of developing angina pectoris, a hereditary condition in my family. For a few days, the very slightest physical effort left me nearly dead. Just getting up from an armchair demanded a huge effort.

I was sitting in such an armchair just opposite the superb view I had on the lake and the French mountains beyond, inwardly grumbling about this condition, when suddenly something (which I cannot explain, it was like an immense inner power) propelled me up like a rocket, with arms wide open in a V shape, and I just said *yes, yes, yes* out loud to absolutely everything that existed in or entered my life, starting with my symptoms. I was instantaneously healed: all my energy flowed back, and I threw myself into my home-cycling practice with the same energy and enthusiasm as before as if nothing had ever happened.

This experience was so powerful that in the following years, when I walked in the street, I would say a silent yes on every third step, and finally, I published the book mentioned above on the great *yes* to all life.

TOWARD A SPIRITUALITY OF SERVICE

With the growing world consciousness that all things are linked on our planet, from the microscopic life-forms on land and in the sea, to the eight billion humans alive today—and that our behavior as a race has a huge impact on our environment and the climate, it is less and less conceivable that a spirituality worthy of the name be lived without a strong dimension of service. And more and more, a new vision that is cropping up on all sides is affirming that my neighbor *is* myself, whether he or she lives on the other side of the world or next door, given that all forms of life are the infinitely diversified expression of the same Love that animates absolutely everything.

This present-day spirituality takes numerous forms, from the spiritual healer available 24/7 and who takes calls any time of day or night (I have personally known quite a few) to the social activist committed 100 percent to a cause he believes in totally, from the monk spending long hours in daily meditation to the well-known spiritual teacher who attracts large crowds, to the single working mother trying courageously to fit a spiritual practice into her impossibly crammed schedule.

If we live a spiritual life concerned about the planet and *all* its inhabitants, this may well imply profound changes in the use of our time and money and in our lifestyle. In the new vision, the idea that one possesses one's time and funds (whatever their origin) and is the master of one's lifestyle belongs to another era. We start managing the totality of our lives, all that Infinite Love entrusts us with—our health, our income, our contacts, our time—as if we were simply the stewards of all of these and no doubt many others. The notion of private possessions becomes almost comical.

Personally, I am still only at the beginning of this path of nonpossession, but already it has given me a magical inner freedom.

And let us remember in this time of world crisis that we are all together the stewards of our little blue planet. Will we live up to the trust the universe has in us?

Q *How do I react to the challenges in my life? Do I react with calm and or do they tend to unsettle me?*

Q *How do I use my unique skills to help humanity face the immense challenges of today's world? How am I helping to build a new humanity?*

6

Different Spiritual Paths

SPIRITUALITY CAN BE LIVED in different modes; of which a few key ones follow.

THE PATH OF THE INSTITUTION

Here we are speaking of spiritual practices organized around a specific place (temple, church, synagogue, mosque) and sacred books like the Qur'an, the Bhagavad Gita, and many others, a community of believers that upholds the institution financially and otherwise, the transmission of a specific teaching from generation to generation. This is the case in Islam, Judaism, and Christianity, which are the dominant religions in the West, although Buddhism is rapidly gaining more adherents.

The advantage of this approach is that it offers the seeker a spiritual home, not to mention a real community, which is most reassuring in the atomized world in which we live. However, a weakness of this path, at least in the case of Christianity, is that because of the very static nature of many churches and the rigidity of their teachings, such institutions adapt very slowly to the modern world (as, for example, illustrated by the debates on abortion in many American churches and political circles) and have great difficulty keeping their younger members, let alone attracting new ones.

THE PATH OF THE COMMUNITY

There are many spiritual or intentional communities where people live together in the spirit of cooperation and friendship, dedicated toward a common goal; they can be found by searching the Internet. Below are three examples.

Findhorn in Scotland was probably the first ecospiritual community in the world when it was founded in the sixties by Eileen and Peter Caddy, and it has had an important international influence.

Namaste Village in Ajijic, Mexico, is a vibrant spiritual community founded by *New York Times* bestselling author James Twyman. The community draws from the spiritual teachings of many traditions that are centered on an individual awakening to our oneness with God. The primary focus are the principles found in the Unity Movement, as well as many other nondual paths.

Ananda Village is a global spiritual movement, based on the teachings of Paramahansa Yogananda, bestselling author of *Autobiography of a Yogi,* who showed how everyone can realize God in their daily lives as a tangible, loving reality. Swami Kriyananda, a disciple of Yogananda, founded Ananda based on the belief that the world needs a blend of the best qualities of the East and West: the spiritual insight of the East and the practical efficiency of the West. The Ananda community is situated on nine hundred acres of meadows and forests amid the foothills of the Sierra Nevada Mountains in Northern California.

THE PATH OF THE SPIRITUAL TEACHER OR GURU

Examples in this field are extremely numerous. One well-known figure is Omraam Mikhaël Aïvanov, a Bulgarian teacher who founded the Fraternité Blanche Universelle (Universal White Fraternity—absolutely nothing to do with race!), based on the teaching of another Bulgarian giant, Peter Deunov. Among many teachings, Deunov predicted that humanity would enter a new era characterized by a much stronger collective consciousness.

Another very well known teacher of Indian origin is the aforementioned Paramahansa Yogananda. He spent many years of his life teaching in the United States, and twenty days after his death, his body still showed no signs of decomposition.

One cannot avoid mentioning Amma Sri Karunamayi, an amazing figure, known the world over. Her simple message is based on universal, unconditional love. Amma is famous for having given hugs to tens of *millions* of people all round the world. Neither a preacher nor a guru in the classical sense, she is the incarnation of her message: living unconditional love and disinterested service. She received the Nobel Prize in 1999, and her life is a living example of her basic message of interbeing: we cannot live alone; we live through our relations. Her whole life has been dedicated to alleviating the suffering of the poor. When asked the source of her incredible energy, she replies: "Where there is true love, anything is effortless."

Another contemporary example of a guru with a worldwide impact is the teacher of Jamaican origin, Mooji, whose home base is Monte Sahaja, a monastery in Portugal, where he hosts numerous classes and retreats. He is a disciple of Papaji, who was a devotee of the revered Ramana Maharshi, one of the spiritual giants of India in the last century. Mooji received his training at the Sri Ramana Ashram.

Mooji radiates goodness and love and also has a wonderful sense of humor. He has a very important spiritual message based on feeling our true spiritual identity, which has nothing to do with the little ego that most people assume is their identity. One can receive via e-mail his free short, daily videos in English, on the Internet.

The Choice of a Spiritual Teacher

There can be important advantages to having a master or a spiritual guide for those who feel they need such a support. Here are three important ones:

1. The transmittal of a lived example to the teachers' students.
2. The transmission of a specific teaching, which hopefully gives clear indications on how to orient oneself in this

increasingly complex world. For example, I frequently follow the daily videos of Mooji.

3. Finally, certain spiritual teachers can transmit to the disciple powerful energy that, in some subtle way, can help open up his or her consciousness.

Personally, after following for close to forty years a very rigorous teaching, among others on spiritual healing, I left the practice. (The only reason I did not leave earlier were the amazing spiritual healings I received for thirty years.) Now I am very clearly on a nondualist spiritual path best represented by Joel Goldsmith, the founder as already mentioned of The Infinite Way (which is also the title of his main book presenting his teaching). I find Mooji a considerable help, too, as his nondual teachings are impeccable, especially concerning our identity, one of the two or three fundamental issues of the spiritual path. However, the great challenge of such relationships is to avoid putting one's master or teacher on a pedestal and making all sorts of projections onto him or her.

THE PATH OF MOVEMENTS AND GROUPS

Spiritual movements are numerous in today's world, and to attempt to make a list of them with even just the briefest definition would cover pages. However, I believe that a sincere and motivated person will sooner or later find a movement or group that suits him or her.

An alternative to an institutional affiliation would be to create your own support group or spiritual activity. For instance, many years ago I created in Geneva a blessing circle where twice a month we met to bless people and world problems. This group was totally informal, but the warmth and love among the members was very real. The group became for me almost like a family, and I felt infinitely more at ease there than in the movement I had belonged to for almost forty years.

As Sandy Wilder, founder of the Educare Unlearning Institute in Grafton, Illinois, says in a small poem:

One Thing

If I could remember just this one thing
I believe I would be free once and for all:
I do not run my life.
Life knows what it is doing
At each moment.

For many years Sandy has been daily sending out such brief and original messages, 365 days a year. They are of great value and have nourished me daily for many years.

THE PATH WITHOUT OUTSIDE GUIDANCE

These are people who are traveling on a spiritual path without being attached to a group or a specific teaching and who are constantly receptive to anything that could broaden their spiritual horizon and open their heart. It is clearly impossible to have the slightest quantitative data as to their number, but my sense of things is that their numbers are rapidly increasing with the dissemination of a growing number of teachings thanks especially to the Internet. Never in history has the human race had at its disposal such an incredible tool as the Internet, which makes the totality of human knowledge available anywhere on Earth as long as you have a good Wi-Fi connection.

This path clearly has its risks, as do probably all the others. One is winding up on a dead-end road, not knowing what to do next, or being drawn into a movement with a sectarian tendency.

In one of his daily videos, Mooji makes an extremely important point for all seekers: "Spirituality cannot be taught, it can only be discovered. It cannot be taught as what is taught goes into the human mind. It has to be awakened in you. . . . The mind cannot understand it. . . . The greatest step towards a life of happiness and simplicity is to let go. Trust the power that is already caring for you spontaneously and effortlessly."

That is the word that every spiritual seeker must cherish, inscribe in their heart—*trust*. Once more we are not alone on our path. We are guided by a Source far beyond anything we could ever imagine. Remember, as we live in an infinitely benevolent universe, sooner or later everything, absolutely *everything*, can only work out for our highest good.

THE PATH OF THE
INDIGENOUS NATIONS

The U.S. government and Christian churches spent more than 150 years trying to eliminate American Indian spiritual practices. But the spiritual beliefs survived. Across America, Native Americans, young and old, are returning to traditional ways. There are well over five hundred indigenous tribal groups in the United States with their own cultures and practices.

The spiritual leader of each tribe is called the *angakut* (or shaman, to use a term more common to most readers), and he plays an important healing role in the community. Most if not all indigenous spiritualities see the entire universe as being alive, which explains the great respect these peoples have for the natural kingdom. There is a belief in the basic interconnectedness of all natural things and forms of life with Mother Earth. Their daily (often private) practices frequently include sacred objects.

Below is an excerpt from *The Soul of the Indian* (Eastman 1911) by Charles Alexander Eastman. Eastman (1858–1939), born Hakadah and later named Ohiyesa, was a Santee Dakota physician educated at Boston University and a writer, national lecturer, and reformer. In the early twentieth century, he was a prolific author and speaker on Sioux ethnohistory and American Indian affairs and worked to improve the lives of youths. He founded thirty-two Native American chapters of the Young Men's Christian Association (YMCA) and helped found the Boy Scouts of America. Eastman is considered the

first Native American author to write American history from
the Native point of view.

The Great Mystery

The original attitude of the American Indian toward
the Eternal, the "Great Mystery" that surrounds and
embraces us, was as simple as it was exalted. To him it
was the supreme conception, bringing with it the fullest
measure of joy and satisfaction possible in this life.

The worship of the "Great Mystery" was silent, solitary, free from all self-seeking. It was silent, because all
speech is of necessity feeble and imperfect; therefore the
souls of my ancestors ascended to God in wordless ado-
ration. It was solitary, because they believed that He is
nearer to us in solitude, and there were no priests autho-
rized to come between a man and his Maker. None might
exhort or confess or in any way meddle with the religious experience of another. Among us all men were created sons of God and stood erect, as conscious of their
divinity. Our faith might not be formulated in creeds, nor
forced upon any who were unwilling to receive it; hence
there was no preaching, proselytizing, nor persecution,
neither were there any scoffers or atheists.

There were no temples or shrines among us save
those of nature. Being a natural man, the Indian was
intensely poetical. He would deem it sacrilege to build
a house for Him who may be met face to face in the

mysterious, shadowy aisles of the primeval forest, or on the sunlit bosom of virgin prairies, upon dizzy spires and pinnacles of naked rock, and yonder in the jeweled vault of the night sky! He who enrobes Himself in filmy veils of cloud, there on the rim of the visible world where our Great-Grandfather Sun kindles his evening camp-fire, He who rides upon the rigorous wind of the north, or breathes forth His spirit upon aromatic southern airs, whose war-canoe is launched upon majestic rivers and inland seas—He needs no lesser cathedral!

That solitary communion with the Unseen which was the highest expression of our religious life is partly described in the word *bambeday*, literally "mysterious feeling," which has been variously translated "fasting" and "dreaming." It may better be interpreted as "consciousness of the divine."

7

Spiritual Tool Kit

JUST AS ALPINISTS CARRY CLIMBING IRONS, ice axes, ropes, and other aids to reach the summit they aim for, spiritual seekers also make use of numerous practices and tools to assist them in their aim of living a dynamic spirituality that inspires them and supports them at each moment.

But before mentioning these methods, I wish to comment on the most important step for any person wishing to follow a spiritual path on which they progress with joy rather than flogging themselves along or telling themselves they should have done better.

Please have for yourself *the most immense tenderness,* an overflowing patience, an unconditional love with which you envelope yourself as with a cape, an instantaneous forgiveness for your lacks and weaknesses. You are on this path solely for yourself, not to please some stern deity that jots down your every failure. The Source does not wait impatiently for you to finally arrive home, as you never left your home in the Source. According to the understanding accepted by a growing num-

ber of people, it is only on the level of the dream that you
made the choice to incarnate on Earth to have the experience
of a material existence with a little ego that believes it runs the
show and has to be answerable to the universe or some dis-
tant and severe deity. You are not accountable to anyone except
yourself, and with gentleness and encouragement, you will do
better.

Too many people in our Judeo-Christian culture have
been raised with the mentality that they must justify all their
actions (and even their thoughts—theologians really know
how to be pitiless!) to a deity who holds an accounting ledger
and even, in too many representations of existence after death,
manages a hell where people will roast forever. As if the Being
of Infinite Love that runs this show called "the universe"
could punish its own creation in such a totally sadistic manner. (This modest book is not the place to enter into the complex history that explains how such passages ended up in the
gospels—the earliest ones of which were written ninety years
after Jesus's resurrection.)

The aim of the spiritual path is not holiness, even if holiness is very occasionally one of its expressions. The aim of the
spiritual path, as I see it, is the fullness of a life lived in radiant joy, a serenity that absolutely nothing can disturb, and
especially unconditional love, which is the greatest gift we
can offer, first and foremost, to ourselves. This is what a great
avatar meant when he stated that the Kingdom of God—that
space of complete fullness and beatitude—is *in* us.

In *Return to the Sacred,* Jonathan Ellerby gives us an

interesting classification of the various methods or spiritual paths:

Approaches centered on the body (ritual and ceremonies, sacred movements, sounds, and music)

Approaches based on the spirit (prayer, meditation, spiritual study)

Approaches based on the heart (devotion, sacred service, following a guru)

Approaches based on the soul (ascetic practices)

As far as I am concerned, I won't attempt a classification, which might be useful for someone doing more intellectual research, but simply mention some methods upon which any person on a spiritual path looking for a method that really nourishes him or her can rely. Trust your own intuition before you bend in front of the authority of well-known teachers or writers, however respected they may be. No one is familiar with the path you have followed until now, with the possible exception of some very close friends, and no one knows your real needs in this area. My choice is subjective, based on methods I have practiced for many years.

MEDITATION

Numerous practitioners, whether teachers or simple pilgrims on the path, would classify meditation as the queen of approaches for those wanting to progress. It has played a key role, especially in Asia. In the West, it is a much more recent practice but one that is spreading rapidly. Many consider it irreplaceable. It is clear that in the ultra-agitated and fast-speed train of our modern society, it can play a key role. As to which style to practice, there is an immense range to choose from, and the best approach would be to try different methods before selecting the one that suits you.

MENTAL DISCIPLINE

For me, this is *the* grounding of all true spiritual practice, and it is the tool *par excellence* on this path. We are all aware that our thoughts are like a young, spirited colt that vigorously resists all attempts to discipline it. This is aggravated by the infernal constant bombardment of our mental space by the media and especially advertising. And it is further worsened by our cell phones, which, for many, constitute the last stage in the daily invasion, not to say rape, of the sacred spiritual center each of us carries inside ourselves.

One statement that has helped many seekers attempting to discipline their young, wild colt is the statement, which has various forms, "To bring every thought captive to love" (or life, God, peace—choose the word that speaks most to you). Personally, this has been my principal spiritual discipline for many years. As a friend wrote to me: "The ego is so cunning and the mind its favorite weapon," and it seems to delight in tricking us moment after moment with totally incongruous thoughts, especially during our moments of spiritual practice.

It is extremely astute in catching on to absolutely anything in our environment to distract us from our aim—which is why earlier on we stressed the importance of perseverance. This is why the discipline of constantly bringing your thoughts back to a key concept like love or peace is so helpful.

An additional powerful tool is the practice of blessing, which I present in chapter 8. This practice is very different from the often very formal religious tradition that the term usually refers to. It is one of the most efficient methods to master the young colt.

Another practice, which is one of my favorites, is choosing a certain number of key topics to which you return at certain fixed times of the day.

And of course, there is the use of a mantra: a brief expression, often just a word or two, that one uses constantly throughout the day. Consider, for example, the story of Saralah and his "Always You" from chapter 2. Mantra is one of the most important spiritual practices the West has imported from India and is now practiced all round the world.

REGULAR PAUSES DURING THE DAY

This practice is extremely important for anyone traveling the spiritual path. It is very simply the practice of regular pauses of a few minutes during the day. Some manage to make them every hour, others every two hours. You freely choose your frequency. There is even a wonderful app you can put on your cell phone called "Mindfulness Bell," which is an extremely helpful tool for any person wishing to seriously discipline his or her thoughts or simply reconnect for an instant with the divine center.

PRAYER

Traditionally, the way of praying in practically all the religions and spiritual practices of the world consists in asking something of an often faraway deity (somewhere "in heaven," wherever that is), counting on the deity's goodness to accept our demand favorably.

In the imagery of my childhood Sunday school, this representation was a bearded old grandpa sitting on a cloud and distributing his favors to those who had behaved obediently. With minor variants, the practice is similar almost everywhere, asking for what one wishes—and the asking can go on for many, many years. That was my approach for most of my existence.

What follows is my adaption of a prayer attributed to the Buddha. I suggest you read this prayer very slowly, pausing after each sentence. Above all, you have to feel the prayer in the heart. For example, take the first sentence: "May all beings be happy." Try and feel that happiness intensely, wishing it from the bottom of your heart, and try and visualize any group you wish to pray for (alcoholics, the native populations of the Amazon, those on death row everywhere or just in your country). A prayer that is not felt has no more impact than an article on a football match read in the local newspaper while sipping your coffee. Only a *felt* prayer heals.

May all beings be happy and feel at ease.
May all beings feel joy and be secure—all.
> *Without omitting any be they in the high,*
> *medium, or lower spheres of existence,*
> *be they modest or important, visible or*
> *invisible, close or far away, born or waiting*
> *to be born.*
May all beings, everywhere, be happy and feel
> *at ease.*
May no being deceive or despise another being,
> *whatever their condition.*
May no being—be it due to anger or a bad
> *intention—wish evil for another.*
And as a mother watches over and protects
> *her only child, in that manner we should*
> *cherish without limit all beings, radiating*
> *an unlimited goodness on the whole world,*
> *above and below and all around.*
And may all people cultivate unlimited
> *loving-kindness and compassion for the*
> *whole world, that it may be free from all*
> *malevolence and hostility.*

A modern form of prayer, which is very frequent today and which was invented two thousand years ago by a great avatar called Jesus, is visualization. His statement "Whatever you ask for through prayer, believe that you have received it and it will come to pass" (Matt. 21:22, translated from the French Louis

Segond Bible) could be called the first expression of the technique of visualization. It really can be called a modern form of prayer, which agnostics or even atheists can practice. For what is prayer if not essentially a sincere request or demand; prayer is a simple desire.

Let's give an example of how visualization works. Your daughter Abigail wishes to become an apprentice in a flower shop. You could formulate your request in the following manner, always ending with an expression of gratitude, which is the most powerful manner of "sealing" the visualization: "Thank you, universe, the dream place for Abigail is already awaiting her. Thanks for the abundance of good you wish for all your children." You could add "awaiting her and all girls in this city." It helps if you can include the senses—the fragrance of the flowers in the shop, the gentle tinkling of the doorbell when a client enters the shop.

Personally, I abandoned the traditional form of praying many years ago and have replaced it with silence. Seek silence as much as you can on your spiritual path because it nourishes us in a very special manner, especially in this society where our mental space is constantly and aggressively invaded by so many forms of useless noise and commercial sales pitches, which I call mental hammering. Authentic silence already reigns deep down inside us, and only the aggressive invasion of our mental space by this insane environment of modern life prevents us from being aware of this. We spoke earlier of that great healer, the American writer and spiritual teacher of the last century, Joel Goldsmith. I have already mentioned that when he received a request for help, the first thing he did was to forget the name of the person concerned and the problem that needed healing and plunge into the inner space deep down inside his consciousness. At that moment when he felt that on the level of "real reality" (for want of a better term) all was already OK, perfect, healed, the work was done. I once reached this state with the already mentioned experience of infinite love on the airplane, and it was the most extraordinary moment in my whole existence. Goldsmith describes this process in his book *The Art of Spiritual Healing* (a book I have read four times!).

Sandy Wilder, the aforementioned founder of Educare Unlearning Institute, says it so well in one of the daily meditations he sends out into the world every day.

A Minute of Singularity

Everything comes out of silence
and then goes back into silence.
What if you provided an invitation
each day for the noise in your mind
to go back to that from which it came?
One way to do that
is to give your mind a single object
to follow instead of the
cacophony of random thoughts and feelings.
The simple beauty
of following your breath
is that it is singular,
and between each

inspiration and expiration
is this Space of silence and stillness.
Drop into this even for one minute.
Watch what discontinues,
and the soothing balm which arrives,
as you are re-embraced by
the Ground of Presence.

THE PRACTICE OF
THE DIVINE PRESENCE

This practice is one of the most elementary and simple and efficient practices of the spiritual path as it simply consists in feeling the divine presence at any time of the day, in any place, and during any activity. One of the briefest and most splendid books on this theme is the already mentioned great classic *The Practice of the Presence of God* by Brother Lawrence (numerous editions in many languages), who was a cook and cobbler in a monastery of Carmelite monks in Paris in the seventeenth century. His practice simply consisted in being always conscious of the divine presence, and his kitchen was transformed into a place where he conversed constantly with God. One might classify this practice as a variant of mindfulness, a spiritual practice that has spread all over the world and about which information is easily available. And however one defines or classifies the practice is of almost no importance compared to whether one does it or not!

THE PHYSICAL PRACTICES

For me, the fundamental criterion for evaluating all spiritual practices or tools is the following question: Does it enable me to grow in love? As this is for many the ultimate aim of the spiritual path.

One has to be very careful concerning all body-related practices, since abuses are numerous in this field, such as various forms of self-mutilation or physical punishment. Such practices are not only totally useless but even counterproductive and demonstrate contempt for that fabulous divine creation represented by our body and such a profound lack of self-love.

Some practices are, of course, useful, such as yoga or fasting, if practiced with moderation and not as an end in themselves. I practiced fasting one day every week and some longer ten-day fasts with great ease for many years, and such practices give one a precious sense of control: I govern my stomach and not vice versa. Yoga, tai chi, and qigong have a spiritual origin and purpose and are not just an Eastern variation of gymnastics.

8

Healing through a Practice of Blessing

THIS CHAPTER IS ON THE PRACTICE of blessing, but a form of blessing that is very different from that practiced by the priest or pastor who raises his arms at the end of a religious service and blesses his flock, wishing them divine grace.

This renewed sense of blessing, which came to me in one of the most challenging moments of my life, consists in sending focused love to a person or situation anywhere. It gives a deep joy to the whole of life when it is practiced consistently. In addition, it is an amazing healing tool, especially, but not exclusively, in the field of human relations. (See the Gentle Art of Blessing website: gentleartofblessing.org.) It has helped a good many overcome depression, as mentioned in the healing described below. Discovered through a huge trial of mine, it has become a canticle of joy in my life and that of many thousands across the world.

In the eighties, I was working for a group of Swiss NGOs

that operated in the field of Third World development issues. They all had programs in Third World countries, and I had been asked to start an information program for schools on these issues. I was highly motivated in my job to the extent of having a camp bed in my office for the nights when I worked late and missed the last train home. My sponsors were aware of the fact that I had refused a lifetime contract with a much higher salary with the Swiss Ministry of Foreign Affairs for the extremely modestly paid job they offered me.

I very much wished to organize a roving exhibit for schools on the theme of hunger, still today one of the major world problems: in 2019, one in nine people suffered from some form of chronic malnutrition, and figures are increasing in a world that throws away one-third of its food production! But my sponsors told me to drop the idea as they did not have the funds. As I'm not the type to scrap a good idea just because someone is raising a red flag, I decided to fund it with my personal savings. This represented a very large sacrifice for me and had evidently never happened in the experience of the four organizations concerned. The exhibit was entitled "Ending Hunger Today" and was very favorably spoken of in the press.

At that time, I had also become a volunteer in the Swiss branch of a world campaign against hunger, the Hunger Project, which had started in the United States. The slogan of the campaign was "end hunger by the year 2000," which I adopted with enthusiasm as it was also the slogan of an African farmers organization in Senegal, with which I entertained warm relations from my work with the aforementioned

Association Internationale 6-S in Burkina Faso. I used this slogan in my work with schools and the roving exhibit.

However, the head of one of the four sponsoring organizations for which I worked, and to whom I once had told that I got up at 4:30 a.m. to meditate, was also—unbeknown to me—a militant atheist. Therefore, he decided that such a crazy fellow like me should not continue working for them. I was summoned to a business meeting of the four representatives of these NGO organizations by this gentleman. No minutes were taken, and I was told that either I stopped using the slogan of the Hunger Project in my work with schools, or I should quit my job.

I could have started a huge row over the affair, even in the press, but decided to quit—the only possible stand to stay true to myself. As quitting was my decision, they did not have to give me any compensation and neither was I eligible for any unemployment benefits. I was without a job for thirty months before I started my personal development workshops, which have been a source of unending joy for thirty years.

However, after leaving my job, I developed a huge resentment toward this gentleman, my former employer, which was literally destroying me. (Resentment is a horrible feeling to harbor—it's like a rat gnawing at your entrails!) It inhabited me very literally from the minute I woke in the morning till the last moments of my day. It was quite unbearable—and unending. I was reading all the right texts, chanting, using mantras and prayers—nothing worked. The beast just enjoyed free camping.

Then one day, reading the Sermon on the Mount, one statement hit me like a strike of lightning: "Bless those who curse you." But of course, Pierre, it's so simple—you just have to bless them. And that's what I started doing: from morning till night—nonstop. I just blessed the persons involved in their health, their joy, their work, their abundance, their peace, and their trust. And the rat in my entrails started shrinking.

Then, one day in the street, quite spontaneously, I started blessing passersby. Then in shops and restaurants. On public transport (still today one of my favorite places to bless! I have no car). I used to walk the whole length of the train both ways to be sure to miss no one. And I started seeing amazing things happen: "impossible" situations transformed in the twinkling of an eye because I was silently blessing all those concerned.

One day, I was writing the text of a speech I was supposed to give at an international youth meeting in Zurich on the theme "Healing the World," when I suddenly received an inspiration as never before or since in my existence. The following text (Pradervand 2009) just flowed to my mind, and I felt like a scribe under orders. Since then, this text and the video crafted by our wonderful webmaster, Jane Young, have literally touched hundreds of thousands of people and can be found on the Gentle Art of Blessing website.

The Gentle Art of Blessing

On awakening, bless this day, for it is already full of unseen good, which your blessings will call forth; for to bless is to acknowledge the unlimited good that is embedded in the very texture of the universe and awaiting each and all.

On passing people in the street, on the bus, in places of work and play, bless them. The peace of your blessing will companion them on their way, and the aura of its gentle fragrance will be a light on their path.

On meeting people and talking to them, bless them in their health, their work, their joy, their relationship to the universe, themselves, and others. Bless them in their abundance and their finances . . . bless them in every conceivable way, for such blessings not only sow seeds of healing but one day will spring forth as flowers in the waste places of your own life.

As you walk, bless the city in which you live, its government and teachers, its nurses and street sweepers, its children and bankers, its priests, and prostitutes. The minute anyone expresses the least aggression or unkindness to you, respond with a blessing: bless them totally, sincerely, joyfully, for such blessings are a shield which protects you from the ignorance of their misdeed, and deflects the arrow that was aimed at you.

To bless means to wish, unconditionally, total, unrestricted good for others and events from the deepest chamber of your heart: it means to hallow, to hold in reverence, to behold with utter awe that which is always a gift from the Creator. He who is hallowed by your blessing is set aside, consecrated, holy, whole. To bless is yet to invoke divine care upon, to speak or think gratefully for, to confer happiness upon—although we ourselves are never the bestower, but simply the joyful witnesses of life's abundance.

To bless all without discrimination of any sort is the ultimate form of giving, because those you bless will never know from whence came the sudden ray that burst through the clouds of their skies, and you will rarely be a witness to the sunlight in their lives.

When something goes completely askew in your day, some unexpected event knocks down your plans and you burst into blessing: for life is teaching you a lesson, and the very event you believe to be unwanted, you yourself called forth, so as to learn the lesson you might balk against were you not to bless it. Trials are blessings in disguise, and hosts of angels follow in their path.

To bless is to acknowledge the omnipresent, universal beauty hidden to material eyes; it is to activate the law of attraction which, from the furthest reaches of the universe, will bring into your life exactly what you need to experience and enjoy.

When you pass a prison, mentally bless its inmates in their innocence and freedom, their gentleness, pure essence, and unconditional forgiveness; for one can only be a prisoner of one's self-image, and a free man can walk unshackled in the courtyard of a jail, just as citizens of countries where freedom reigns can be prisoners when fear lurks in their thoughts.

When you pass a hospital, bless its patients in their present wholeness, for even in their suffering, their wholeness awaits in them to be discovered. When your eyes behold a man in tears, or seemingly broken by life, bless him in his vitality and joy: for the material senses present but the inverted image of the ultimate splendor and perfection which only the inner eye beholds.

It is impossible to bless and judge at the same time. So hold constantly as a deep, hallowed, intoned thought the desire to bless, for truly then shall you become a peacemaker, and one day you shall behold, everywhere, the very face of God.

P.S. And of course, above all, do not forget to bless the utterly beautiful person YOU are.

I started sharing this text in my broad international correspondence, and a close friend of mine, president of one of the largest medical associations in the United States, started doing the same. I began receiving letters from people everywhere sharing their enthusiasm and explaining how the practice of blessing had resolved umpteen kinds of challenges. Some are mentioned in my basic book on this subject, *The Gentle Art of Blessing*. The practice has been tested in some of the most impossible situations in the world, from death row, Texas, which is the end of the road leading to hell, to some of the poorest villages in the world in Mali, West Africa.

Personally, it took me three years of daily blessing to overcome my resentment toward the person who had conspired to make me leave my job (followed by two and a half years without income as I had "voluntarily" quit my job in the view of the unemployment agency). But I had already started receiving testimonies of the efficacy of blessing to heal relationships and other challenges.

Ten years later, at a meeting on development issues, I faced my former tormentor. Amazingly, I felt inside me an explosion of joy such as never before in my life. I felt like hugging and kissing him! We decided to go and have dinner together and the whole time my heart was singing, singing, singing. Not one word on what had happened to make me lose my job. And I realized that our encounter was a perfect illustration of the paragraph from my text on blessing, which states:

> When something goes completely askew in your day, some unexpected event knocks down your plans and you burst into blessing: for life is teaching you a lesson, and the very event you believe to be unwanted, you yourself called forth, so as to learn the lesson you might balk against were you not to bless it. Trials are blessings in disguise, and hosts of angels follow in their path.

I now have the deep belief that this man and I had made a soul contract before coming on Earth. According to this belief we make a certain number of contracts with people before incarnating to play certain roles in given situations. The incredible joy that I felt (and that lasted quite a few days) was due to this awareness, as this practice has enabled many, many thousands all around the world to transform difficult and sometimes impossible situations into paths of learning.

BLESSING IN DROUGHT, HUNGER, AND VIOLENCE

In Mali, near the city of Mopti, are villages harassed by constant droughts, the Muslim jihadist fighters, and permanent hunger—I have been in regions where people were eating the bark off trees to survive. A very dear friend from that region, Mamadou Kassambara, founded a small NGO to help the population survive. In this extreme desolation, Mamadou spends his time blessing. Here is the extract of a letter of his written in the summer of 2020:

> It is now more than three months that, in addition to tap water, the supply of electricity is irregular. The population manifested so that the problem be solved. The problem of security is more than preoccupying. Already a very short distance from the city one cannot move without taking great risks.
>
> Every day God grants us, in this region, one observes slaughters, tragedies in full daylight: dozens of deaths every single day. . . . Here we witness misery in all its

forms without a touch of poetry, an unprecedented hate and tragedy . . . that we experience here on a daily basis. No one can say with certainty if he will still be alive in an hour. . . . To this tragedy one has to add the COVID-19 pandemic, the terrible disease of the century. . . .

At a time when the great majority of those who kill do not know why they are killing, and those who are killed do not know (in their majority) what they have done to deserve death, there can only be one solution: blessing!!! Nothing else but blessing can meet the sufferings facing all humanity. I am convinced that with blessing I will be able to recover my trainers* and will be able to take them back to their families, if it is the will of God. I repeat: absolutely nothing but blessing can relieve an individual, a group of people, a whole nation. It is the only remedy we have against all diseases and vicissitudes, against all forms of violence. . . . Yes, the only worthwhile one. However, this miraculous tool called blessing has a prerequisite as you stress: intention, which carries it and leads it to its destination. Without such an intention, blessing leads nowhere. First you have to love and forgive, and then you have to love blessing.

Without forgetting constancy in perseverance, endurance, tolerance, and patience. It cannot happen all at once. One needs patience in one's constancy in blessing at every moment.

---

*Some of Mamadou's trainers from his NGO had disappeared—kidnapped or killed by the Muslim jihadist fighters.

Here is a person who lives a daily hell, both he and his whole region—and who spends all his time blessing.

Of course, many readers will understandably have difficulty connecting with remote areas of rural Sahel, but maybe Texas rings closer to home. Texas death row is certainly one of the closest places to hell in the United States: six-by-nine-foot cells with a tiny slit just under the ceiling to let in the light.

BLESSING ON TEXAS DEATH ROW

At the time Roger McGowen wrote the following quote (early 2000s), breakfast was served at 2:30 a.m., lunch early morning, and dinner early midafternoon. On good days, inmates had an hour of exercise in a tiny space with cement floor, walls, and ceiling. Food did not include at the time any fresh fruit or vegetables, and violence and noise were constant (impossible to sleep more than three hours in a row). When they were submitted to collective punishment, inmates were secluded in their cells with just peanut butter sandwiches. Many inmates become crazy, and in recent years, 4 percent committed suicide. The functioning of the Texas legal system is so abysmal, especially for African-American inmates, that inmates have been known to stay twenty, thirty, or even more years on death row before being exonerated. There is no community activity—inmates spend their days in total solitude and some never ever have a visitor. Others who have no more contact with their families (which was Roger's case) do not have a penny to spend for the minimal survival tools on death row: a coffee pot and a small radio. There is no chaplain on Texas death row. Some inmates executed have been later recognized as innocent, and since the eighties, 185 inmates were exonerated after being held for years under the menace of death.

Sometime after receiving my blessing text, Roger wrote:*

I have to tell you, Pierre, how your text on blessing helped me. I constantly keep it with me. Since we have been moved to this prison, the officials have been trying to associate me with one of the prison gangs. I have no idea why. They have no reason to even suspect me of anything like this. I have always carried myself with respect, I have never fought or threatened any of the officers. I was on death row at Ellis One Unit for fourteen years before coming here, and there never was any sign of gang activity on my record, because I do not belong to any gang, unless Christ is the gang leader. But upon coming to this prison, they have taken upon themselves to make me a gang member in four months and they have been making my life a living nightmare.

Much of my personal property has been destroyed, and they tore my cell apart twice a day.† They tore it on

---

*The quotes from Roger's letters in this chapter are all from my book *Messages of Life from Death Row.*
†In prison jargon, this is called a shakedown: two prison guards come along, handcuff the inmate, and put him in the corridor in front of the open cell and then enter and create sheer bedlam—tearing book covers, pouring ketchup on family photos or even destroying them, and so on.

December 23, my birthday. They came back and did it again on that same night. They tore it apart again on New Year's Eve, they really destroyed things that day. . . .

I was upset, really upset. I was so upset in fact that I stopped talking to anyone. I wouldn't even answer the officers. I would just come out of the cell, wait till they tore it apart, go back inside and just sit in the middle of the things thrown everywhere.

Then I received *The Gentle Art of Blessing* and began to read, and my burden began to lift.

I closed my eyes and told God that I did not know what lesson I was supposed to learn from this. I knew he would not allow me to suffer like this without cause. So I started blessing the officers, all of them, especially those who had just torn apart my belongings. And I realized that God was showing me the calm in the middle of the storm, and that love is so easy. Like the Polish lawyer in your book who decided not to hate the Nazis after witnessing the death of his family at their hands, I will not bow to hatred. They cannot make me hate them. I will continue to bless them, regardless of what they destroy, because they cannot destroy the love that I have for them as children of God. I have to forgive them a thousand times the harm they do. I will not be a victim. Blessings for others are blessings for us. God never forgets. When we bless others, we also bless ourselves, mind, body, and self.

Actually, things have gone smoothly over the last month, and I recognize it is because of my blessing everyone all day and night, no matter who they were or what they have done to me. I love *The Gentle Art of Blessing*. . . . Yes, things are a lot easier here, not because the officers have changed but because my outlook has changed. I look at things with a renewed sense of love and understanding . . . I no longer look at myself as a victim of these people's assaults. I now look at myself as a divine being able to accept any- and everything, and to love everyone, because I am a "product of love" and I search for the lesson in all things.

From the Sahel to Texas, a spirituality that sings in the midst of the storm.

HEALING DEPRESSION AND NEGATIVITY THROUGH BLESSING

What follows are a couple of healing examples of this spirituality, drawn from the section "Healing testimonies" on the Gentle Art of Blessing website. In one, a German Swiss supermarket employee, through blessing, heals his depression—one of the most frequent and intractable health problems of the contemporary world.

After my burnout, I had to give up my job as chief of a subsidiary of a supermarket chain. Thanks to drugs, a stay in a clinic, and psychotherapy, I tried to put together the pieces of my life and in the past year I had started my work again in a subsidiary of the same supermarket chain.

But constant mood swings brought me very close to a relapse. Depression and negative thoughts had again started controlling my days. Mid-December 2014 I had an appointment with my psychiatrist, Dr. J. Do you know what he recommended to me? Not the drugs that I had stopped taking for some time. No, instead he prescribed two books. Your book *The Gentle Art of Blessing* and *The Power of Now* by Eckhart Tolle.*

I recently finished reading the two books and can see in them the solution to all my problems. . . . These books show me a path that I can follow to give me my zest for life back.

I have started blessing absolutely everything—even my burnout. Maybe the illness was showing me that I needed to change my lifestyle, that I needed to live more consciously and follow another path. It is the opportunity for me to reconnect with happiness and love and to reconnect with them and specially to share them.

Since I have started blessing—and believe me, in my work there are numerous opportunities to bless—negative thoughts are receding, the past is less present, and I feel better every day.

A difficult twelve-year professional relationship was healed through blessing. Ann, a participant in one of my workshops

---

*For a Swiss psychiatrist to do this is like the president of the United States suggesting that the country adopt pure communism. The practice of medicine in Switzerland is very heavily drug oriented.

on blessing, was a teacher in an average-sized grade school, and she had a colleague who ignored her completely. For this person, Ann simply did not exist. Each time their paths crossed, she turned her head in the other direction. Ann had not the foggiest idea why her colleague treated her this way, behavior that perpetuated year after year. Twelve months of such behavior would already be unpleasant—but twelve years?

So Ann decided to start blessing. Day after day, she poured out blessings on her colleague. Results were soon manifested. Just before a school holiday, her colleague came up to her with the most beautiful smile and wished her a wonderful vacation.

THE BLESSINGS OF FRIEDA

Here is my favorite blessing story, taken from a German Swiss newspaper, *Tages-Anzeiger* (April 15, 1999). It concerns a retired nurse, Frieda, who felt led to undertake a really surprising task—although *mission* would be a more appropriate word. In the busiest section of Switzerland's main train station in Zurich, Frieda, who had a disability, would stand for *fourteen hours a day,* supporting herself by leaning a hand on her wheelchair, simply blessing the passersby. She did this six days a week for *over ten years*. She refused to give the slightest interview, saying simply that she felt called by God to undertake this task. Her example touched me in a special way because her definition of blessing is exactly the same as the one in my blessing text: wanting the real good of persons, events, situations, and so on. (One can find an eight-minute video of Frieda blessing people on my Gentle Art of Blessing website.) Only a superhuman power can have enabled this disabled retired person to fulfill her mission for at least ten years. If one estimates that she blessed ten persons per minute, with pauses, that adds up to around eight thousand per day or a little over two million per year—for ten years. (Frieda should posthumously receive the Nobel Prize for blessing.)

Her impact on the globe might ultimately be more important than some of those the media call the movers. As a great avatar said, "The first shall be the last and the last the first."

You too, my friend, can bless anyone, anytime, anywhere, all the time.

An army of anonymous Friedas transforming the world.

Why not?

Afterword

DEAR READER: may your path be one of discovery and joy.

It is my deeply held belief that within a generation or two, a spiritual practice that creates and reinforces links between humans and the planet will have become the norm in the whole world. For on this shrinking globe, either we manage to create this win-win world that works for all (the environment included, of course) or it will no longer work for anyone. And spirituality will have a key role to play, possibly *the* key role.

And to touch large strata of the population, including modestly educated populations with limited means, this spirituality will need to be simple to practice and down to earth.

Blessing as the sending of focused love is an example of such a practice, but there are, of course, many others.

So from the bottom of my heart, I can only wish you a safe and uplifting journey; whether it is serene or turbulent, it will open for you, if you persevere, unforgettable green pastures that absolutely no other practice or discipline can offer you, with the promise of sooner or later reaching your goal.

So, friend, be blessed on your travel,

It is my dearest, heartfelt wish for you.

Vaya con Dios.

Bibliography

Caplan, Mariana. 2009. *Eyes Wide Open*. Louisville, Colo.: Sounds True.

Desjardins, Arnaud, with Veronique Loiseleur. 2000. *L'audace de vivre*. Paris: Pocket.

Don, Megan. 2011. *Meditations with Teresa of Avila: A Journey into the Sacred*. Novato, Calif.: New World Library.

Dubois, David, and Serge Durand. no date. *Guide de la spiritualité: Les meilleures adresses pour trouver son chemin dans la spiritualité contemporaine*. Paris: Almora Editions.

Eastman, Charles Alexander. 1911. *The Soul of the Indian*. Boston and New York: Houghton Mifflin.

Eddy, Mary Baker. (1865) 2015. *Science and Health with Key to the Scriptures*. Boston: Christian Science Publishing Society.

Ellerby, Jonathan. 2009. *Return to the Sacred: Pathways to Spiritual Awakening*. Carlsbad, Calif.: Hay House.

Ellul, Jacques. 1986. *The Subversion of Christianity*. Grand Rapids, Mich.: Eerdmans.

Goldsmith, Joel S. (1947) 1984. *The Infinite Way*. Longboat Key, Fl.: Acropolis Books.

———. (1970) 2002. *Seek Ye First*. Longboat Key, Fl.: Acropolis Books.

Ferrucci, Piero. 1991. *Inevitable Grace: Breakthroughs in the Lives of Great Men and Women*. New York: Tarcher.

Kolodiejchuk, Brian. 2007. *Mother Theresa: Come to My Light*. New York: Doubleday.

Lawrence, Brother. (1895) 2016. *The Practice of the Presence of God.* Mansfield Centre, Conn.: Martino.

McGowen, Roger, with Pierre Pradervand. 2012. *L'audace d'aimer: Une voie vers la liberté intérieure.* Geneva: Jouvence.

———. 2017. *Messages de vie: Un condamné à mort témoigne.* Geneva: Jouvence.

Pradervand, Pierre. 2009. *The Gentle Art of Blessing.* New York: Simon and Schuster.

———. 2009. *Le grand oui à la vie.* Geneva: Jouvence.

———. 2009. *Messages of Life from Death Row.* Charleston, S.C.: BookSurge.

Quentric-Séguy, Martine. 1998. *Au bord du Gange.* Paris: Seuil.

About the Author

Pierre Pradervand studied at the University of Geneva, the University of Bern, and the University of Michigan, Ann Arbor, before receiving a doctorate in sociology from La Sorbonne University in Paris. A true world citizen, Pierre has labored most of his life for social justice—living, working, studying in, or visiting forty countries on every continent.

From his Geneva home, Pierre is now active as a writer, speaker, and life coach, helping people to live simpler yet richer, more contented lives. He provides personal development tools that empower attendees to strengthen their internal anchors and advance on their spiritual path. Pierre is also an independent celebrant for weddings, burials, and other events. He is the author of more than twenty books.

Index